Sacraments for Secular Man

Sacraments
for Secular Man

George McCauley, S.J.

Herder and Herder

1969
HERDER AND HERDER NEW YORK
232 Madison Avenue, New York, N.Y. 10016

Nihil obstat: Leo J. Steady, Censor Librorum
Imprimatur: ✠ Robert F. Joyce, Bishop of Burlington
January 24, 1969

Library of Congress Catalog Card Number: 69–17698
© 1969 by Herder and Herder, Inc.
Manufactured in the United States

Contents

To My Jesuit Brothers

Sacraments for Secular Man

Introduction

In its opening message the Second Vatican Council spoke of the Church's desire to build up the city in this world. It is not my purpose to catalogue the complex reasons why an opposite impression got abroad, namely, that the Christian life had little to do with this world. The impression is not a new one. Tacitus reports that Nero found an easy handle against Christians in their "hatred for mankind" (*odium humani generis*). It is at any rate a fact that the council felt obliged to correct such an impression and to affirm the Church's place in the secular city.

But one senses that the council's convictions are not generally shared. Many wonder about the relevance (that word!) of the Church to the contemporary scene. The experience Christians are trying to communicate supposedly includes and goes beyond every manifestation, every nuance of enthusiasm, altruism, sensitivity and yearning that *this* world has ever known. Yet where in the Church is there a sense of excitement? When we are not perplexed about recent developments, we are often boring, to ourselves and to others. Our internal and external reforms are often so somber, ponderous and reluctant that one hesitates to entrust one's energies to them. We seem constantly to be retooling to produce what is already obsolete. Attempts to be creative and imaginative in catechetics, liturgy, theology and pastoral work are often viewed as gross accommodations to the prevailing mood; or are attributed to the personal whim of their authors. Is the reason for all this because we are unaccustomed to think of our faith as rooting us in a city in this world? Perhaps.

11

At any rate it seemed useful, in this introduction, to place this study of Christian sacraments in a context which would relate them to the contemporary theological task of finding the Church's place in the secular city. We are in a period of theological slogans: demythologizing, secularization, radical theology, aggiornamento, personalist anthropology, religionless religion and even de-theologizing. Whatever the value and legitimacy of these slogans, it seems clear that they, together with the council, are talking about the city in this world. They are concerned with human problems as we experience these problems: "What is man? What is this sense of sorrow, of evil, of death, which continues to exist despite so much progress? What is the purpose of these victories, purchased at so high a cost? What can man offer to society, what can he expect from it? What follows from this earthly life?" (*Pastoral Constitution on the Church in the Modern World,* article 10).

The resolution of these questions can be ignored: John Courtney Murray spoke of an atheism of distraction, which accounts for more people than we would like to admit. Again a solution can be thwarted by what William Lynch calls the romantic imagination, which, by drawing man's attention away from an encounter with this world, contributes to the alienation of man from himself. Others, however, are interested in the city in this world. They are not slow to come forth: scientists, technologists, business men, sociologists, philosophers, lawyers, statesmen. They tell us, "We have lived in the city in this world for some time now, longer than you perhaps. We have a certain amount of experience, some know-how, not the last word, no pipe-dreams; but we are willing to put what we have at people's disposal. We live moderately, but well; there is lots of work, lots of new angles to explore. No pressure, you come in if you want." Many do go in.

And what of our Christian faith? Does it contribute to man's

12

alienation from himself and from his earthly city? Or does it make a man enter into himself and into the city in ways that he would never have dared were it not for the prodding, unsettling, encouraging experience of Christ? This is the question that I would like to pose with regard to the sacraments.

But what can we legitimately expect from a *theological* enquiry into questions like these, whether or not they specifically touch upon the sacraments? For certainly the voices of theologians have not been silent in recent times, to the frequent consternation of many people within the one Church. Partly that consternation is due to the fact that different theologians approach problems with different presuppositions and emphases in procedure; provided everyone is aware of the special stamp of any given theology, such diversity of approach is a healthy thing. Yet not everyone expects, much less encourages this diversity. Not a few are reluctant to accept the fact that there are as many theologies as there are theologians. They confuse theology with the proclamation of the Gospel, or with a catechetical compilation of the high points of traditional Church teaching. They expect or demand that there be one and only one theology, agreed upon by all or certainly by all within the one Church.

For these reasons I would like to explain the approach to the sacraments which I follow in this book.

Theology of itself is not directed at making someone say, "Yes, I believe"; rather, it seeks to evoke the response, "Yes, I understand a little better now." This understanding is called for when questions arise which press us to make sense out of our faith experience or out of the relation between our faith experience and our profane experience. If the question that is posed for the theologian is an historical, philosophical, doctrinal or biblical one, then an historical, philosophical, doctrinal or biblical answer is in order. But more often than not, the question

13

that emerges is none of these. It is, rather: what tangible role does the Christian faith play in our everyday profane experience? Theology, in the most proper sense, seeks a totalizing, inclusive, synthetic understanding of the faith experience in relation to profane experience.

In this book, we will not theologize about the sacraments in predominantly biblical terms. Such a procedure has been popular in the past. We were assured that, in our sacramental actions, we were repeating what Christ himself did. Hence we were encouraged to study the New Testament in order to seek out its understanding of sacraments. But in order to understand what the New Testament was saying about Christ, we had to look farther back into history to the symbols and sacramental gestures of the People of God. For it was their history that found its completion in Christ and influenced the very language and gesture that Christ used to express himself. All this was well and good, but when the weight and emphasis of our explanation depended on such a procedure, we risked missing the main point. The central theological question that is generally posed today is: do the actions of Christ—which we say he continues in our midst, and which we are invited to take part—really speak to *our* human situation?

If the Jewish people had their troubles getting saved, we may or may not sympathize with this fact, depending on whether or not our interest is ever aroused. But interest will normally be aroused to the extent that we are conscious of some unity of situation which binds them to us. At first glance, their situation seems totally different. They seem a narrow, contentious, morbid, idealistic, hypocritical, superstitious, calculating and chauvinistic lot. Of course, that is the whole point. God is the kind of God who deals magnanimously with such people. And all men are, in their own way, narrow, idealistic, morbid, superstitious and all the rest. The sacraments are intended to touch men in these

14

deeply human and sensitive areas, to bring them as they are into the presence of Christ, hopefully and without pretense. But when theologians spend so much time and energy introducing people to the biblical world, often without helping them to identify with it, the result is that men frequently fail to root the sacraments in their soil. Hence, a more direct approach to what is permanently relevant in the sacraments is both necessary and valid. By direct I do not mean that the theologian ceases to learn from scripture. But he does not attribute to scripture any magical efficacy which relieves him of the responsibility of translating for the men of today the biblical view of faith and sacrament. The bible of itself does not necessarily supply the language suitable to a synthetic understanding of the faith.

If our approach will not be mainly biblical, it will however draw upon scripture and tradition. The theologian seeks understanding of complicated questions from a variety of equally complicated sources: an impossible mass of factors to manage. What he normally does is to seek some leverage, some principle by which he may thread his way through his manifold experience without losing his way or his audience. This principle or working hypothesis enables him to map out the terrain in such a way that answers or (more often) gives further dimension to his original problem. This principle may in fact be a truth that he believes with all religious earnestness. It may even, *within definite limits,* be agreed upon by many theologians. But, *as far as its ability to illuminate the larger question at hand is concerned,* it remains untried, and must be called an hypothesis.

In the following study of the sacraments, one central hypothesis will be at work. We may formulate it variously: sacraments are secular gestures; they deal with secular reality; they promote a greater secularity than we are accustomed to associate with human existence; in themselves they embody secular experience; in one sense, an enriched secular experience *is* the grace of the

15

sacraments. It remains to be seen whether or not this hypothesis will stand up to the facts of faith and of profane experience. First, however, we must define what is meant by "secular" in this study.

In current theological literature several meanings of secular are possible. In the first or *neutral* sense secular means whatever addresses itself to the felt problems of human living; it would imply a vital interest in the psychological, social, political, economic and cultural plight and progress of men. This first meaning of secular says nothing, one way or the other, about religious faith.

A second meaning of secular is not so neutral. In this second case, which we will call *antireligious secularity,* a vital interest in man implies the exclusion of any interests that are "religious" or "metaphysical." Needless to say, the proponents of this second kind of secularity have often constructed caricatures both of religion and of metaphysics from out of this meaning. The same could be said for much of what has been written about "Hellenism" and "scholasticism." Many antireligious secularists regard themselves to have been liberated from a religious tradition that stifled their (neutral) secular concerns. Yet is it not true that very often the case here is that of a later generation misreading what an earlier one wrote, of grossly miscalculating the demands of scholarship? Not infrequently the theological reading public have to pay for their initial literal-mindedness.

A third meaning of secular is possible: that implying the same sort of humanistic concern which is found in the neutral secularity described above, but where it is further assumed that *religious faith has a role in developing humanistic concern.* Faith in an incarnate God becomes the impetus for man's appreciation of his own incarnate situation.

In some theologians, however, it is not clear how long that

16

role will last. In this fourth or *ambiguous* view, religious faith seems to have a sort of built-in, diminishing half-life. A process is envisaged in which more and more human activities will gradually cease to be carried out in the name of God or of Christ or of a Church. God (and Christ) is in fact supposed to will this process. His desire is to hide himself and so to withdraw from the conscious motivation of men that ultimately we have nothing left but men conscious of their responsibility to do the God-thing without the God-consciousness implied in religious faith. But if it were some sort of religious faith (God-consciousness) that set off the process of secularization in the first place, it would seem more logical that, the more God disappears from consciousness, the *less* secular we would all become. We will return to this question in a moment. For the present, I will try to describe in what sense I am putting forth the hypothesis that sacraments are secular gestures.

I would certainly not accept the formal exclusion of faith contained in the antireligious sense of secular; and yet I would include the humanist concern of the neutral sense of secular. But the neutral sense does not, as we pointed out, deal with the question of how religious faith in general influences or relates to secularity, so some honest attempt must be made here to describe that influence and relationship. It is all too easy to escape this task by introducing a purely *temporal* dimension into the meaning of secular and so defining it as "that which occurs before death." This emphasis on the temporal is valid and it is certainly needed where so many people look on religion solely as a waiting-chamber for the next life. But to be in favor of this kind of temporal secularity does not solve all the problems. In fact, if applied to the sacraments, it would be sheer tautology, since Christians do not foresee the use of sacraments in the next life anyhow. The real point at issue in discussing the secular is not the question of this life versus the next life. It is rather the

17

relation between faith and a concern for human development. Does faith (in Christ, in God) draw our attention away from this development or not?

Those who accept the fourth kind of secular concern mentioned above are ambiguous when they speak of this relationship between faith and human development. They insist that the *whole* point of religious faith is to turn our attention to secular living. If they are Christian secularists they argue that God, by becoming incarnate in Christ, showed how serious he was about the secular creation which he has initiated as a gift to men and which he clearly wants them to enjoy. Moreover, they would argue that the ascension of Christ, after which he appears no more among us, has this same object lesson in view, namely, to send us with insistence and encouragement to the tasks that are before us. While there is some truth to such an analysis, the fourth type of secularity, as I said, does not make clear the continuing status of God and of the risen Christ. A number of death-of-God theologians at any rate contend that there is no continuing relationship possible between man and God or between man and Christ. It is the plan of God, apparently in their view, that God cease to be on man's mind, or that he cease to be *simpliciter*.

In my opinion such a view has serious limitations. In the first place it embodies the same view of God-the-Big-Planner that in the past set about so many useless controversies concerning God's providence. Instead of demythologizing such a view of God, secularists of the fourth kind simply substitute another Big Plan drawn mostly from the analogy of the efficient, invisible, production-minded corporation executive of today. In thus conceiving of God, they have depersonalized him to the extent that they also deny the possibility and desirability of his continuing communication with men.

18

What, then, is a proper view of Christian secularity in which both human development and religious faith are adequately respected? I would offer the following formula for Christian secularity: it would attempt to honor the impetus given to human growth by religious faith but would insist that a continuing possession and affirmation of that faith is necessary for adequate human growth. Descriptively, it would say that the Christian who is attentive to the secular is *not alone* in his attentiveness. He looks at and lives in the secular *with* God, *with* Christ. He affirms (by faith) that God is with him. He affirms that he can address him as *you* in what we call prayer. He is neither logically nor psychologically forced by such affirmations to conclude that all eventual conversation with God will be *about God* instead of about secular realities. By the same token, a man and a woman deeply in love with one another do not usually shun the hard realities of life. Neither does the conversation which continues with God in Christ by religious faith necessarily require that we uproot ourselves from our secular ground. In this sense, prayer is the point at which all theologies of secularity either stand or fall.

If we focus for a moment on the sacraments and examine the relation there between religious faith and secular concern, it becomes clear how difficult it is to defend the position I have just taken on the meaning of Christian secularity. For in much of sacramental living we lose sight of the secular realities involved. We receive the sacraments for extrinsic (in the secular view) reasons: to fulfill the conditions set down by divine *fiat* for some eschatological salvation; to perform dutifully what is required by some divine plan. Such reasons, insofar as they neglect the secular reality of the sacraments, seem to me to lean in the direction of that "magical view of the world" which Vatican II urges Christians to be rid of. On the other hand, we must maintain that sacraments are religious gestures, that is, that without losing their identifiably human dimensions they are open to the kind of prayer-conversation with God in Christ which distinguishes an authentic Christian secularity.

Due to this tension between a valid desire for secularity on the one hand and the necessity for prayer on the other, the general question people ask about religious faith itself becomes the specific question they pose about the sacraments: why bother? I am convinced that this question can be advanced with all sorts of false expectations on the part of those who raise it. To some it means: make it easy for me to live with the dialectical tension between faith and secularity. For others it means: *prove* to me that Christ is present in sacramental living. Still others mean: *give* me faith. To anyone who seeks to fulfill the latter three requests I say good luck. I do not think that it is possible solely by talking to get such persons "to bother" about the sacraments.

In my own view, the question "Why bother?" is raised for another reason: many people conceive of God and of God's relationships with man in such a way as to *exclude any reasonable expectation* that in religious faith there is the possibility of conversing with God about secular realities.

Let me illustrate this key point of our presentation. The most persistent misconception men have of God, one that refuses to die out, is that God stands to gain something from his contact with men. One of the reasons why many people feel that God is a distraction from, or a threat or hindrance to secular realities is because they associate God's actions in human life with some sort of accumulative evolution *in God himself.* They think that the successful human execution of God's plan is a condition of God's own security and happiness. This pursuit of God's own perfection must, of course, render anything that happens to man, anything secular therefore, of secondary importance. But the glory of God, revealed to us in Christ, is that he *gives* of his

20

fullness, in an ineffably unselfish and unself-conscious way. In his dealings with men God *has to* be man-centered, and even creative in man's regard. God does not make man in order then to enter into a kind of personality contest with him. And yet men often are dubious of God's altruism. They are suspicious of his gifts, and they project their own motivation onto him, making him the Great Competitor.

There is a second difficulty that people have when they try to relate religious faith and secular concern. This centers around the fact that sacraments are described as *supernatural* and *graced* realities. Now each of these terms is perfectly valid and meaningful within a very definite and limited range of signification. However, their signification belongs within the categories of cause or explanation, not within the categories of what we would call, especially in a religious context, familiar experience.

At the risk of explaining what is unclear by what is less clear, we may draw a parallel between these categories of the supernatural and grace on the one hand and the philosophical notion of transcendence of the other. Bernard Lonergan has said of the latter that, "despite the imposing name, transcendence is the elementary matter of raising further questions" (*Insight,* p. 635). The questions the philosopher raises lead, upon intelligent inquiry and critical reflexion, far beyond our familiar experience. The philosopher is constantly extrapolating from this familiar experience, but at no point of his intelligent inquiry and critical reflexion is he pretending to *describe* experience in the normal sense of that verb. Hence to base a criticism of philosophical conclusions on the fact that they do not *describe* all that they *affirm* is to miss their point completely. We cannot expect the philosopher to do what he is not claiming to do, that is, to speak only in the concrete terms of describable experience.

If we apply this point to the matter of grace and the supernatural, we find that these too are *affirmed* in the course of *ex-*

21

plaining a more primary and more familiar experience. They are not intended to be *descriptions* of that experience. The experience in question is, of course, the conviction Christians have that their insertion into the Christian life is a *gratuitous* act of God in Christ.

It is true that the term "grace," as it is used in the scriptures, *describes* this conviction. But the elaboration of a theological theory of grace was never intended to be descriptive in the scriptural sense. Neither was the term "supernatural." In the context of a theological elaboration, we affirm that grace and the supernatural render intelligible our primary Christian experience. But intelligibility here is relative to the kind of "further question" asked about gratuity. We are in no way claiming to measure the intelligibility in question by our power to describe grace in concrete terms and language. Hence we should not be deceived by these terms when they reappear in sacramental theology or in preaching. We should not suppose that we are witnessing some new *kind* of describable human experience. If our lives are graced by God, this means on the *descriptive* level that in our human life we take on a new attitude, namely awareness of and gratitude for God having addressed himself to us in Christ. In the technical, elaborated sense, however, it means something else. It means that our new awareness and gratitude are tracked and charted, as it were, according to an intelligible model by which we represent to ourselves God's activity in our regard; thus, for example, "created actuation by uncreated act." It does not mean that the *human mode* and *style* of our life changes. I do not say that our conduct does not change. But, it remains a recognizably *human* conduct. We have simply raised a new question about that changed conduct.

Thus to affirm that sacraments are supernatural or graced realities does not impel us to introduce into our lives a kind of anxious falsifications of our selves. Our faith-conversation with

God does not require a change in intention, vocabulary, posture, dress. I suggest that the obsessiveness attached to many such mannerisms is due to a well-intentioned attempt to keep one's actions "graced" and "supernatural" in some descriptive sense. This not only need not be so; in the proper technical sense of those terms, it cannot be so.

The purpose of this introduction has been to set forth the limited project before us and to show how and in what sense that project is theological. In effect, what we will be trying to do is to strip down the sacramental system to a skeletal structure in which the basic secular affirmation which the sacraments contain will stand forth. We do this not in order to see whether the sacraments work—for we normally strip down something only when it ceases to function properly, but to see *how* they are a part of the Church's engagement in the city in this world. It is an undeniable fact that our sacramental theologies have hardly begun to take account of the secular side of the sacraments. If the Incarnation is *the* great secular act, we must draw from it all the many subsequent implications for Christ's sacramental gestures. We must attack all forms of sacramental Docetism. The role of faith in our task is fundamental, faith which "throws a new light on everything, manifests God's designs for man's total vocation, and thus directs the mind to solutions which are fully human" (*Pastoral Constitution on the Church in the Modern World,* article 11).

1.

Affirmation

In the sacrament of baptism, which they perform in the name and at the bidding of Jesus Christ, Christians affirm life at its deepest secular levels. The traditional description of baptism as the "gateway" indicates well how baptism is an initiation into a new way of life. But this gate opens out onto city streets; it opens out onto God involved here and now with our lives—and not only out onto heaven, for then baptism would be an initiation into a life foreign to what is secular.

Yet to love life, to affirm it in the face of its violent rhythms, is an arduous, perhaps an heroic feat. A great number of people, caught up in the rude exhilaration of their daily job or finance or politics, never even reach the point where they can consider such a task. Others fear it; some withdraw from it; some are defeated by it. But to succeed in exposing oneself to all its form and lines and textures and sounds and colors, and then to give it affirmative expression in one's own life, is an achievement of the highest order. It is an achievement requiring the labor and joy of the true artist—who, Christians insist, Jesus Christ is.

When New Testament writers speak of baptism, therefore, they emphasize the fact that it makes us heirs of God with Christ. The term "heir" is a felicitous one. The heir is one who *feels* at home; he *belongs*. But as Paul points out, the Christian is already, in some positive sense, at home in this secular life. The lot that has befallen him, his incredible good fortune, is something which begins in this life and which affects his attitudes towards this life. His hopes go beyond this life, not by contempt for it, but because he bluntly recognizes that he is not up to fully accepting the gift of sonship here and now. For he is quick to embrace the forms of slavery which he himself or others invent. Thus there is always tension as he tries to love, in all secular things, the God of the secular—who will *still be* the God of the secular even when we see him face to face. We cannot dispel this tension by introducing into our lives an exaggerated opposition between secular life and life beyond.

Such are the broad dimensions of the Christian's affirmation of life. We are talking here of a global affirmation, of a basic attitude, of a Christian's "gut-reaction" to life. The Christian community is affirming in baptism that the threat which secular life poses has been radically lifted with Christ. All subsequent fear and trembling of Christians is not to be directed against secular realities themselves, but rather against being separated from Christ in whom they have found the courage to be what they are, to love where they are, to be at home with themselves, to belong.

We must now examine what "affirming life" entails. We must also examine in greater detail why this affirmation of life is attributed to the community, and how the individual relates to that community. But these further analyses will be useless if we are unable to recognize from the start that man is someone who moves more by broad orientation, by global impulse, than he does in terms of individual choices. If he has his bearings he can move ahead; otherwise he dissipates his energies and wanders. In baptism, we maintain, man receives such a basic orientation.

That is why the symbol of water is aptly used in this sacrament. It is sometimes said that religious symbolism is no longer really effective. The use of water in baptism is offered as an example: city boys are familiar only with the practical uses of water. They cannot appreciate the richness of its symbolism. Somehow water cannot conjure up for them an insight into the complex possibilities of life; it cannot convey to them the promise of renewal beyond all the amorphous, day-by-day wear and tear which life exposes us to; it cannot express to them the feeling that life in all its secular rhythms is to be a refreshing, sustaining experience.

But the fact is that baptismal catechesis is usually given to *small* boys. City-raised or not, their problem consists not in not understanding the symbolism of water but rather in not appreciating the existential situation to which this sacrament addresses itself. How can we expect them to grasp a multivalent symbol like water, which is quite suited to describe a basic life-orientation, when they have little or no idea of what a basic life-orientation is?

Religious symbolism is, in this respect, no different from any other kind of symbolism. If we isolate it from a life-experience, a symbol becomes stale and boring. This is true even of the so-called natural symbols which recur in many and varied cultures. Only if we see symbols in a lived context will they strike us powerfully. Fellini, for example, has had remarkable success with water as symbol. In *La Strada* the sea offers a running commentary on the lives and fates of the protagonists. At one point they return to the seashore. Gelsamina flies, birdlike, to the water's edge. She is renewed, not only because the sea is her childhood home, but because she brings to the sea the small handful of joy which she has found in the brute Zampano, and which she has been able to integrate into her tiny spirit. Zampano, on the other hand, plods into the shallow waters and urinates. Everything has been said, but not by the sea alone. The symbolism of the sea is effective only when it is artfully worked

27

together with the real-life problems of the protagonists. If someone is uninterested in their fate, he will never be interested in the symbols used to express that fate.

That which should shape our thinking and appreciation of the sacraments is, beyond the material symbols used, the words spoken. Or rather, the discourse that takes place, since the words only have meaning as part of a discourse between persons about someone or something. As we have already suggested, the *something* about which Christian baptism is discoursing is a basic orientation towards human life. Baptism is also talking about *someone,* and it is from this latter point of view that we will better be able to approach, in closer detail, what kind of basic orientation the sacrament of baptism envisages.

The baptismal formula in itself is quite severe: "I baptize you in the name of the Father, and of the Son, and of the Holy Spirit." But it is intended to be evocative, implying the wider discussion in which Christians speak to one another about Christ, and speak to the risen Christ about life. What is the picture of Christ, and of his attitude towards life, which is present in the baptismal discourse? Christian teaching has insisted on the fact that, in baptism, we are *introduced into the death and resurrection of Christ.* This truth is certainly central to the doctrine of the sacrament, but in themselves the death and resurrection of Christ are, as it were, "bald facts." As such, they are without significance, because significance presupposes a signifier. To arrive at the precise significance intended by Christ in these events is a task requiring the constant reflection of believers—reflection, and not simply repetition, because simple repetition does not advance our understanding of the relationship between Christ's death and resurrection and our contemporary discussion of baptism. We have suggested that baptism commits the Christian to the secular realities around him. We should now show that the *death and resurrection of Christ are also a comment on these*

28

secular realities. Only in this way will our interpretation of baptism as an affirmation of life respect the doctrinal and liturgical language used by the Church to speak of baptism.

But in what sense can we say that the death and resurrection of Christ were an affirmation of life? That they were a work of art? Was not his death a sordid affair with nothing to commend it and much to condemn it? And was not the resurrection in a sense too abrupt, too obscure, too other-worldly to have anything to do with an affirmation of secular life? Such questions will seem insoluble if we so isolate the death and resurrection of Christ as salvific events that we fail to see their continuity with his constant motivation and his lifelong conviction. It is as the *final* embodiment and *full* expression of Christ's *constant* convictions about life that the passion and resurrection become for us, in baptism, the source of our own affirmation of life. In his death and resurrection, as in his whole life, Christ showed a radical willingness to let freedom in, to let people in, to let hope in, to let God in. All are consequences of one another, each implies the other. Heinrich Schlier has shown, for example, how Christian freedom is not simply a matter of autonomy or even a kind of fidelity to one's personal development. In *Man Before God,* he writes, "For the ancients, liberty meant freedom to rule oneself, whether in the political or in the philosophical sense. It was defined as independent dominion over oneself. But freedom in the Christian sense can be defined as putting oneself at the disposal of others. This sort of freedom was 'folly' to the Greeks, whom we take for the very prototype of man." Hence Christian freedom is a freedom which opens an individual to other persons. It therefore implies community, and hope too, for even our glorious liberty, in its *concrete* manifestations, often resembles a groan of longing (Rom. 8, 26). For Christians, then, there can be no such thing as freedom at the expense of other people, nor any such thing as freedom to the exclusion of other people. The

29

freedom of Christians is precisely to be, like Christ, open to other people. Baptism, in which we make Christ's own affirmation of life, is thus more than an introduction to cult and to a Church; it must necessarily move the Christian and the Church beyond cult, for it orients the Christian to the mission of Christ to the world—to all men, all cultures, all secular reality.

Yet might it not seem that such statements are somehow a little too pat? Have we assigned to baptism perhaps too secular a dimension, since who among us can really take up Christ's offer to be open to all men? For one thing, the problem of secularity is not whether we should or should not bestow "Christian value" on technology, art, or science. These human accomplishments, by their own power, demonstrate their own value sufficiently well. The real issue is living in the same world with the people who labor in this technology, this art, this science. By our baptism, we have said, we are open to them all. In baptism, we affirm that this openness is possible, desirable, and will never, all appearances to the contrary, be radically ineffectual. Yet does this not all come down to a kind of mindless gregariousness, to naïve community-mindedness, to lack of creative selectivity?

The answer to this objection, if there is one, lies in the fact that, while baptism proclaims the kind of universal love which motivated Christ throughout his life, it proclaims that love as something which is to be defined and achieved according to the historical circumstances in which the Church finds itself. Baptism is a call to life, an invitation to universal love. But the concrete implications of that call and the spelling out of universal love must be worked out by the Church who tests its own historical experience against the invitation made to it by Christ. There is nothing surprising in this fact. Even Christ himself, however inclusive his love for men was in its motive, had a limited sphere of operation. His mission to the Jewish people was itself occasional. His confrontations were with religious leaders rather than political ones. He distinguished between his close followers and friends and a group of disciples who occupied his interest less. This is what his universal love *looked like.*

In our case, the possibility of men achieving brotherhood is real and baptism celebrates this possibility. But there is still work to be done, with each generation developing a concrete program for brotherhood. What we are faced with, then, is the necessity of knowing to the fullest extent possible the signs of our own time. This does not mean simply that Christians examine how they should apply an evident principle of charity to their historical and cultural milieu. The principle of charity itself is in a real sense opaque. It does not become evident until history gives it concrete shape and form. And this historical learning process operates not only from within the Christian community but from without it as well. As the Second Vatican Council pointed out, we can learn from non-Christians not only what they are, but also what we are, what the contemporary shape of our affirmation of life should be. A concern for racial justice, for world hunger, for peace, is not something which we deduce from our baptismal vows. These concerns are rather things which, by reason of our baptismal community, we recognize more readily, hold more steadily before our conscience, and act upon with greater solidarity.

Hence the objection that baptism presents an unreal picture of man is true, but only in the sense that man does not realize what shape his *commitment to community* should take except by living in an historically rooted community. This is what he takes on by baptism. He affirms that Christ is with him when he takes on the business of brotherhood. He enters a spirited community, one which approaches the problems of community in the enthusiastic spirit of Christ. The view of community which baptism effects is to be a creative process calling upon the wit, energy, insight, and staying power which all worthwhile artistic processes demand.

It is not immediately clear in our own day what the shape of community should be. How much *anonymity*, for example, should the Christian expect in his community? Harvey Cox captures modern man's need for and insistence upon anonymity in his *Secular City*. But anonymity can also disguise our lack of concern and commitment. Or again, how much *selectivity* can there be in the individuals whom the Christian community accepts or rejects, in the causes the community espouses? Can the Christian community ever accept the bitter selectivity we call war? How and by what concrete steps is the Christian community to further the integration of racial, sexual and enonomic minorities into the larger community? We are normally frightened by variety and are tempted to reduce it to some safe and shapeless sameness. But does this quite normal tendency sufficiently respect a legitimate *diversity* within the one baptismal community? What diversity are we to expect and to welcome in the Christian community? All these questions simply bring us back to the realization that the shape of our baptismal community is something that we are still working out. What seems incontrovertible is that our concrete baptismal community is the historical milieu in which things get worked out if they are to get worked out at all.

But another objection can be raised against the kind of community affirmed in baptism: that it does not seem to work. The Christian community does not provide the human resources required for an affirmation of life. Do individuals in fact find a decisive attitude towards life in this community? Is not their individual capacity to affirm other people often better activated by psychiatrists, by philosophers, by sociologists, than it is by baptism? Many people seem to experience great disappointment

32

when a secular salvation for them as individuals is not forthcoming by virtue of their adherence to Christ.

Now partly this objection stems from a petulance which in effect wants some sort of individualistic salvation apart from any consideration of other people. But tradition is clear on the point that the effectiveness of the sacraments is consequent upon their signifying capacity. In other words, sacraments "do" what they "say they will do." If baptism says it *introduces* man into a community *through which* he is fitted out for the communal secular tasks of life, then that is what it does. It does not promise any private sort of salvation. We should judge its effectiveness by what it says it will do. Furthermore, baptism does not say it effects community magically. Man is free under grace. He may choose, therefore, not to be free in the Christian sense of being open to others. Hence no individual should suspect that the promise of Christ has failed him if in fact the promise of Christ to him involves a multiplicity of other freedoms. The success or failure of baptism should not be judged by whether or not an individual is vaulted automatically and without further ado into the advanced stages of interpersonal openness. The baptized person is called to freedom in a community which in itself is in process of a gradual acquisition of Christian freedom. We should not be deceived by the abruptness of Christ's words in the Markan sequel "He who believes and is baptized will be saved." A difficulty with our religious language is that it announces goals and future fulfillment as though they were accomplished facts. Christ's freedom is not so contagious that it cannot be checked by men and even by Christians. One can never be rid of the role of human freedom in building community. In this sense baptism orients us to still another secular virtue—a civility which maneuvres through the *possibilities* of failure in order to work out the community which it believes Christ makes possible.

33

There is no doubt that one is subject to numerous hindrances large and small in this task. Most of the problems stem from confusion between community and regimentation, and from an incredible desire to keep up the appearances of community when no significant effort to make community is present. At times these hindrances may seem for an individual to be so insoluble that he then prefers to seek a *kind* of community different from the one which the Church envisages or a *way* of achieving community different from the way which the Church espouses. Yet the desire to form community, Catholic theology teaches, *is* the desire for baptism. Nonetheless, of all communities having the potential for forming community in the world, the Church claims to be the best equipped. Argument on this point can be endless. Perhaps the Christian can best say to someone who denies this claim, "All right, but if that is your view, go form community elsewhere, but include everyone, respect the necessity of consensus, work to discover the dimensions of love in our time, display that decisiveness of purpose which we too seek to have. With that we can have no complaint."

It should be clear at this point that the Christian definition of freedom is rather unusual. It means to be enabled to love others. It does not bother too much about traditional emphasis on freedom of choice. It presupposes freedom of choice, and it would admit that one can choose not to love others even after one has accepted the Christian definition of freedom as a freedom. But it insists on the fact that Christians maintain freedom to love others is a fitting description of human freedom; more than this, that freedom finds its most apt expression in the Christian community, because that community cherishes the connection between freedom and open-ended love.

This explains why Christians find nothing scandalous about the practice of infant baptism. In infant baptism, it is maintained, the "freedom" of the child is violated by the fact that the Christian community co-opts infants into its company without their being able to choose whether or not they wish to make the same affirmation of life as the adult community. This criticism could stem from several more basic assumptions. It could be simply resentment that Christianity claims that man becomes himself through Christ and through living in community, which in turn is made possible by Christ. There is no way to deal with this resentment except by pointing out that everyone has, in fact, basic assumptions about what man is and how man becomes what he is to become. Freedom of conscience should be respected in Christians too. However, as we suggested, criticism of infant baptism more often is based on the fact that the child is not given the conscientious *choice* of accepting the definition of man which is contained in the Christian idea of freedom. This criticism rests, therefore, on the view that freedom of choice is primary. To this it can be only answered that freedom of conscientious choice is primary only *where it is possible.* It is not possible for infants. Hence in countless ways we make choices for them according to our own view of human life. We give them citizenship, insurance, inoculations, various forms of discipline, health, education, and so on. In giving our children these things we are communicating attitudes toward life with every gesture and word, so much so, according to psychology, that their basic life attitudes are formed before they leave their third year. And we do all this without consulting the infant. Why do we make such an exception of religion? It is because we do not see that religion contains affirmations concerning secular life? Or is it because we disagree with those affirmations?

Criticism of infant baptism labors under a further weakness. It assumes that infants, when freedom of choice does become a possibility for them, cannot reject their Christianity. There is no doubt that people experience great pain and agitation when

35

they reject any part of their childhood patrimony. But this is the normal price that freedom of conscientious choice makes us pay. The choice to abandon one's citizenship or to discard certain family values and attitudes is always difficult. Nor can we make a special category out of religion by saying that the adult Christian is rejecting God when he rejects his baptism. If he has understood his baptism correctly, he should say more properly that he is directly rejecting the community into which he was inserted at baptism. How this step affects his relationship with God depends on the further question of whether or not his judgment that God is not found in his baptismal community is a sincere one.

Throughout this chapter, we have avoided speaking of baptism as an act of prayer in which we communicate with God. This is because, as Schillebeeckx has shown in his work, *Christ the Sacrament of Encounter with God,* the sacraments are first and foremost communications to us from God in Christ. Without neglecting the fact that the sacraments are prayerful actions, it is equally important to realize that our continuing faith-conversation with God is henceforward to take place *in that secular community* to which we have been introduced at baptism. Thus our Christian baptism manifests, as does the Church's whole mission, "a religious, and by that very fact, supremely human character" (*Pastoral Constitution on the Church in the Modern World,* article 11).

2.

The Pragmatist

Puberty is a sign, a portent of nature. It frightens and it fascinates. It is a bluntly physical intimation that man is going to be different from what he thinks himself to be. In what sense will he be different? It is not enough to say that he (or she) is going to be that much harder to handle around the house. Or that his moods, silences, enthusiasms, and other cosmic swerves are going to be harder to interpret and to justify according to some absolute standard of family life and order. It is just this standard that nature is in fact challenging at puberty. For puberty is an intimation made not only to the child but to parents and to society as well. It designates the individual's insertion into the adult community as a responsible agent in that community.

Most societies, aware of the communal implications of coming-of-age, take steps they consider suitable to make the transition beneficial to all concerned. Young people thus are "initiated" into the religious, cultural, economic, and political complexities of the community's adult life. It will do no good having them running about untrained and irresponsible in their newly acquired sexual powers. But more than sexual powers are involved. Sexual coming-of-age is a sign that a young man or woman will soon enter the community, creating new family and economic units, capable of voting, of fighting, of edifying, of enriching, and so on. The intention, or rather the hope expressed in such indoctrination is that the young will profit from the accumulated

37

wisdom passed down to them by the community, so that they will understand the community in a more mature way (and so understand themselves in new ways), and in consequence support and enjoy the community.

Of course, nothing like all this really happens. The adolescent questions many of the standards set by his elders. This challenge from beneath is a healthy thing, because age brings with it the need to justify past achievements, even past mistakes, and to rationalize the methods by which one has come to success. Yet young people, on the other hand, face the rather different temptation of closing themselves off in their own special language, their special clothes, their precious clubs and cliques and friendships, and in these things lived only for themselves there is an unwillingness to live life as it is.

Our point here is not to describe a situation familiar to all, but rather to indicate that what is familiar to all is the subject of sacramental living. In particular, we speak of the problems of transition from puberty to adulthood in order to prepare the way for a discussion of the human element affirmed in the sacrament of confirmation.

Confirmation has indeed been described as the sacrament of Christian adulthood, but this is not the only understanding that people have of it. The popular image of confirmation is that it makes us "soldiers of Christ." This view accepts the soldier as a symbol of maturity, whereas history has taught us that the soldier is a neutral symbol; he can stand for much good or for sheer evil. The whole secondary development in the theology of confirmation in terms of soldier, slapped cheek, and such slogans as "defender of the faith" risks giving the impression of a certain unenlightened pugnaciousness. It gives attention much more to historical circumstances in which the Church found itself than to a permanent formulation of the Christian life.

Perhaps this is the reason why the more prominent formulas

used to describe confirmation today are such as "the sacrament of Christian adulthood" and "the strengthening of the Spirit." This latter formula is intended to describe the relationship of confirmation to baptism. Both formulas, however, are in fact describing the one human phenomenon. Through baptism into the Christian community, we are enabled to make a radical and general affirmation of life in all its rhythms and forms (because we have become sons in Christ and hence heirs of all that is). Confirmation narrows the focus of the Christian's affirmation of life to a more specific situation of life, one which any man normally meets in his progress from birth to death. This is the situation of acquiring adult responsibility.

There are two levels on which we might describe adulthood. On the first level confirmation may be looked upon as that initiation rite whereby Christ's community commits itself to be with the emerging adult as he or she faces the delicate step into an adult world. It is an agonizing thing for a young person to have to learn to view his individuality now in terms of a wider, uncharted network of relationships, institutions, and structures. The community would fulfill this first-level task if it supported the adolescent in achieving mature relationships in those matters with which adult life is normally concerned: the use of money; the role of knowledge and professional competency; relating to the needs of others; coping with ideological pluralism; realizing the contribution that others make to one's own growth; assessing one's sexuality and family responsibility properly. Certainly, instruction along these lines is not the peculiar province of the Church. On the other hand, there is in the Church an accumulated wisdom on mature secular problems such as the above. That the Church should wish to pass on such wisdom is not surprising; and this it tries to do, in part at least, in the context of the sacrament of confirmation.

At the second level, confirmation is intended to communicate

39

to the recipient an adult attitude about the Christian community itself. This proposition will make sense only if one admits a distinction between a more mature and a less mature appreciation of the Christian faith. Such a distinction is in fact affirmed and implied in countless authoritative sources of Christian doctrine. In what follows we shall seek to illustrate from the New Testament the kind of developing awareness and maturing sense of the Christian faith that is envisioned in the sacramental gesture of confirming.

In the Book of Acts there is recounted the growth and extension of the Church through the action of the Spirit. For this reason it is a particularly apt source to explore if we are to understand the "strengthening by the Spirit" that occurs in confirmation. The fact that the growth of the primitive Church is attributed to the Spirit should not, however, lead us to think that its growth was serenely miraculous. There was a great amount of activism among the members of the early Church, and not a few problems. Initially, these problems stemmed from the fact that those who chose the Christian "way" were considered apostates from the Jewish church. They were treated with the usual prejudice shown to religious dissidents: social ostracism, banishment from the synagogue (although they still used the temple for worship), and persecution by Jewish zealots such as Paul, who apparently had limited powers of arrest under Jewish law. The arrests would go on even after the Church moved into the gentile world.

As the apostles moved out geographically into the countries of the diaspora, they were faced with *dogmatic decisions* of no small moment. The dispute over the admission of the gentiles into the Christian community left in each church, factions and parties whose backgrounds differed, and hence whose interpretations of Christian morality were often at odds. Their languages and eating customs, their outlook on law, on the place of women, on secular learning all differed. The Church had to decide basic questions of ritual, sacrament, and faith. It had to forge a unity in concrete circumstances which almost ruled unity out. There is a certain irony to the fact that Luke uses the same language to describe the "growth and multiplication" of the early Church as he does to describe the condition of the people of God in Egypt's slave-state (6, 7; 12, 24).

In his gospel, Luke offers an assessment of how things are going for the Church from the standpoint of *numerical success.* His summations are for the most part optimistic, whereas the events he selects for narration offer little apparent grounds for optimism. We meet venality (5, 1; 8, 18), ignorance of basic doctrine (19, 2), gross misinterpretation of the Christian message (14, 11), some highly suspect compromise and window-dressing (16, 3; 21, 24), and bickering among the apostles (15, 37). And at the end we are reminded—and this reminder is itself an admission of man's radical freedom and radical risk in this saeculum—that the apostolic mission meets with only mixed success: "some believed what was said; and some disbelieved" (28, 24).

In their new pagan surroundings Christians also constituted an *economic threat,* as in the case of the silversmiths at Ephesus. The latter saw their profitable idol-making industry threatened by the new Christian sect. So with the canny Demetrius at their head, the Ephesian smiths succeeded in holding on to their trade for the time being. They did so, of course, in the name of religion: "with one voice for two hours they shouted 'Great is Diana of the Ephesians'" (19, 23).

The first Christians were also a *political problem* for the Jewish leadership and the Roman occupying forces. In this respect, it is interesting to watch Paul's developing contacts with officialdom. At Paphos in Cyprus he won the pro-consul (Sergius Paulus) by working wonders (13, 8). At Philippi he embar-

41

rassed the magistrates by refusing to leave his jail cell in secret as they requested; but later he relented and let the matter drop (16, 35). Gallio, another pro-consul, freed him and threw his case out of court (18, 12). But it seems that Paul was working towards a realization that the issue of the Church's place in contemporary political society must be solved once and for all. For this reason, his return to Jerusalem and the events there were all the more dramatic. In the history of primitive church-state relations, Paul's words to the centurion (22, 25) are climactic: "Is it *legal* for you to scourge a Roman, and that without a trial?" The Church reached, with these words, a startling degree of self-awareness and secularity. For it saw that fidelity to Christ sometimes requires that Christians do certain things and take certain stands that Christ himself would not or did not himself do. Paul sought secular support for his freedom to operate as a Christian, whereas the example of Christ perhaps would have lead him to forego such help from Caesar.

Despite much agitation within and without the Church, the first Christians held up as an ideal, if not as an accomplished fact, a certain unanimity of purpose, even though this unanimity may appear to have been a tenuous one from what we read in Acts and the epistles. But it was a unanimity sufficient to enable the first Christians to speak to their contemporary world with confident outspokenness. No doubt they were only too aware that in their conflicts, scandals, and ignorance they had a poor basis for a mission to the world. But perhaps they were realistic enough in the Spirit to see that their fidelity to Christ required efforts on two fronts, within the community and outside it; not one *or* the other, not one and *then* the other, but both together.

There was a certain utilitarian principle at work throughout this development of the early Church in its search for unity and in its mission to the pagan world. By this we mean that the rights and wrongs, the eventual directions and expressions the Church

42

would take, were not written down somewhere where the apostles could consult them as the need arose. They were surprised by events; they had to read some meaning into the challenge posed to them by opposition, by success, by national and cultural differences. They had to discuss, argue, and decide. They had to discover what faith in Christ should look like in their lives. Their decisions were often anguished ones. They experienced the shock of realizing that the presence of the Spirit of truth in the just man is not much help when every man thinks that he is just.

St. Paul refers to this principle by which the Church was enabled to make the decisions necessary to its growth. "The manifestation of the Spirit is given to everyone for profit" (1 Cor. 12, 17). The words "for profit" are a difficult translation of the Greek phrase *"eis to sumphoron."* Goodspeed translates the same Greek words by "for the common good." The Vulgate has *"ad utilitatem"* which captures better the pragmatic nature of the Spirit's gifts. What is important to realize is that what is given to the apostles and to the other members of the Church by the Spirit for their *utility* is going *to look just like that.* That is to say: as a result of the action of the Spirit, the Church makes decisions in order to forge a *practical* unity and growth in Christ. It fits these decisions to a given time and to given circumstances. As Acts warns us, these circumstances may be unsettling, unexpected, and extremely complex. The Spirit's gift to us is that we work out a solution which is the best practical assessment of the manifold movements of the Spirit in the Church at a given time and place. To attempt to achieve unity in the name of a biblical or dogmatic or theological past *alone* is to abdicate one's responsibility to *utilize* the gifts of the Spirit, who acts where he wills. Rather, as Paul told the Corinthians, there is a pragmatic quality to the Christian's development in the Spirit.

The person who receives the "strengthening by the Spirit" at confirmation has a similar commitment to contribute to practical

43

decisions concerning the Church's life and mission in the adult city. To do so, he is empowered at confirmation with Christ's and the community's insight into the Christian dimensions of adult living. He is called upon, too, to be aware of the adult dimensions of Christian living. We have lived through such a period of paternalism and authoritarianism that the ordinary Christian today finds it difficult to see himself as a factor in this pragmatic decision-making process. Hence confirmation seems to him to be either pointless or a form of personal spiritual hygiene, or a mandate to defend to the death what is thought to be the prevailing consensus of the hierarchy. In a sense Vatican II has said farewell to this period of the Church's history. It employed magnificently the utilitarian principle described by Paul. It paralleled the situation described in Acts (though there were fewer arrests connected with the Council). The issues raised in the Council were not found written down on some mystical agenda. They evolved from the circumstances of the Church's life in the twentieth century. The Council's solutions were practical; they will not please everyone, and they will perhaps be modified or even substantially revised in coming years. But this will surprise only those who look upon the Church as something outside themselves, outside their personal historical needs, discoveries, desires, sinfulness, inquisitiveness, and prayer. It is precisely the role of Christian maturity to break down such facile distinctions between the hierarchy considered as "them" and all others considered as "us." The day will come when children in a family come to accept their parents as other persons, fragile, striving, limited, in need of the experience and conversation of their own children. On such a day, the child truly becomes adult. A day like this must dawn continually in the Church. A vigorous theology (and catechesis) of confirmation as the sacrament of Christian adulthood may be just the practical means to bring about that day.

44

3.

The Conversation

The sacrament of penance is, in its most observable and obvious features, a conversation between Christians about sin. Flowing from this conversation and indeed part of it is forgiveness. Yet it is perhaps true to say that the sacramental conversation of penance has come upon hard times, at least for many Christians. At a time when our moral standards are being either challenged or ignored, it is not surprising that many people are experiencing great difficulty in assessing the moral coordinates of their own individual, concrete existence. Their sacramental conversation in penance thus falls off or becomes disjointed.

We are, too, very conscious today of the ambiguity which conversation can have. Silence, we know, is the privilege of well-aged and tested love. Moreover, words, the carriers of our conversation, can themselves be illusory. We quickly become expert at hiding our true selves behind words. We dissemble with them; we throw up verbal roadblocks which delay entrance into the private citadel of our thoughts. With words we put people off and we lead them on. We pick and choose from among our meager treasure of words to find those which best ornament our pale souls. When we feel threatened, we melt down our treasure to make verbal swords, with which we cut hopes dead or sting another with our hatred. Instead of using words as a means of communicating ourselves to others, we manipulate them to distract ourselves and to fool the world.

45

We might even add that, because of traditional formulations of doctrine and catechesis concerning penance, and because of the assembly-line image that penance has acquired, one often hesitates to admit that conversation has much to do with this sacrament. In traditional terms the sacrament has been described as follows: one person, the penitent, recounts to another, the priest, his sins. In this recounting, moreover, the penitent's attitudes are more or less prescribed. He must be sorry for his sins; he must be resolved against repeating them; he must show a willingness to do something to make up for them. The priest, upon hearing the penitent's account, and upon ascertaining whether or not the required attitudes of sorrow, resolve, and willingness to atone and to amend are present, absolves the penitent of his sins. The absolution is not simply the equivalent of saying to the penitent, "If you believe that your sins are forgiven, they are forgiven"; it is a judgment which the priest himself, in the name of Christ, passes on the sinner. This is a conversation?

In this chapter we will not attempt to justify calling the sacrament of penance a conversation. Neither will we deal with the numerous suggestions that have been made in various quarters to revivify this sacrament by modifying its basic structure, its cultural shape or local circumstances. The problem with the sacrament of penance and with its theological understanding has less to do with such things as these and more to do with certain prevailing notions which psychologically preclude people appreciating the value of the penance-conversation. What are these prevailing notions? They are the notions of sin and judgment as these are actually conceived by many Christians. Our hope is that a theological analysis and review of these two notions is a necessary and perhaps sufficient precondition for the appreciation of the sacrament of penance not only as a conversation but also as a secular conversation.

THE CONVERSATION

We toss off a definition of sin as an "offense against God" without noting that that expression is, in fact, an extremely stylized way of speaking. Taken literally, as most people do take it, it is metaphysical and religious nonsense. By anyone's definition, God is God because he cannot be offended. We cannot say as Christians that our revolt literally provokes a stiffening on God's part, or causes hurt or rage in him. If the expression makes any sense at all it means that man makes an attempt at offending God, that on man's part there is revolt or bitterness. It may also be the case that what we mean by "offense against God" is that man offends, in the proper sense of that word, Christ the God-man. But here too we must be careful. In his divine nature Christ cannot be offended; but in his humanity there are conditions under which—reasons for which—he takes offense. We may *not* presume that they will be the same reasons for which *we* take offense. Christ's human freedom was not threatened by the way men reacted to him. The ignorance and treachery that he was confronted with and the failure and abandonment that he experienced could not turn him from loving his own to the end. He did not root up the weeds the first time they appeared among the wheat; he lets human freedom run its course—which is the most difficult thing that any of us find to do. For these reasons, sin cannot be called offensive to Christ in the sense that it creates in him a personal threat, that it can reduce his mission to failure, that it can provoke in him feelings of revenge or retribution towards the sinner. Where such attitudes are expected, it is obvious that the possibilities of conversation are minimal. Sin, then, is offensive to Christ only to the extent that by sin we throw up obstacles to our sharing his tremendous personal freedom. It was enough to make him weep that people did not listen to him. But his tears are not for himself; they are for all the freedom and love that men will never have without him. In the last analysis

47

sin is an offense against oneself, a curtailment of one's own freedom, a denial of a love that might have been in oneself. This denial includes concretely various forms of alienation from the community and integrity befitting human life. Thus the biblical picture of man's origins describes several kinds of breakdown of community which can be called sin. There is fraternal sin, political alienation, a loss of community with nature and culture, disorientation in matters of sex, and, above all, an alienation from God with whom man ought to have a familiar and trusting relationship.

In describing sin as a failure to love, we are not by that fact saying that love, as a psychological, subjective experience, is the only determining factor in morality. Some proponents of the new morality or of situation ethics would seem to take this view. By love we do not mean the exhilarating inner experience alone, but this experience insofar as it expresses itself in definable external patterns. The norm for the sinfulness or goodness of these external patterns cannot be the inner experience alone, because this latter experience can make mistakes in choosing the proper objects (or even subjects) of its affectivity. Love is and can be blind. But this does not reduce morality to a matter of conforming one's behavior to external patterns of action. These external patterns are ultimately called good and bad because by them we truly respect or deny the multiplicity of freedoms in the world. Where we fail to do so, we have men, in Paul's impassioned rhetoric, "versed in every kind of injustice, knavery, impurity, avarice, and ill-will; spiteful, murderous, contentious, deceitful, depraved, back-biters, slanderers, God's enemies; insolent, haughty, vainglorious; inventive in wickedness, disobedient to their parents; without prudence, without honor, without love, without loyalty, without pity" (Rom. 1, 29–31). For all his catalogues of sins, Paul insists on getting to the heart of sin: sin is to hold back the truth of God; it is to resolve not to possess

48

the knowledge of God. Truth and knowledge of God in Paul's context are the truth and knowledge that God is love; that this love is for all men, to all men; that it is embodied in the redemptive love of Christ for the Church. Christian love is situational, to be sure, but it situates the individual in a Church in which the catholic interests of God and men are served.

It has been a constant theme of Christian theologians that moral evil is not something positive in itself, but is rather an absence of a wider perspective, that of charity. It is sometimes said that we have too long neglected the privative nature of moral evil, the negative effect that evil has on our personality and on the personality of others, and that we should stress these dimensions more. Every sin is basically an unwillingness to be what we might have been. And because of what we have not become, that is, because of our sins, others cannot become what they might have been. That is the way human freedoms interact.

If this is true, what is a person confessing in the sacrament of penance? He is saying that things might have been otherwise and that the fault, if fault there was, lies with his own impoverished, misguided, and selfish misuse of freedom. He is certainly not confessing that he hurt God in the sense that somehow God is put at a disadvantage by our sins. The worst that men could do to Christ was to scourge him and then crucify him. But the whole point of the resurrection was to show that death cannot touch a love that is truly free, truly for all. When Paul says that if Christ is not risen we are still in our sins, he indicates that Christ's resurrection nullifies our sins. How does it do so? By undoing the bodily harm done to Christ? Yes, but even more by affirming that Christ's freedom is now and forever the valid creative force in a world where we find it very difficult to respect freedom in ourselves and in others. Moreover, in instituting the sacrament of penance, Christ did not remain indifferent to man's need to talk about his past lack of freedom. He implied, rather,

49

that it is essential for man to speak about his personal freedom-gap. This human need is attested to by groups as diverse as bartenders and psychiatrists. And so the Church need not apologize for having a permanent forum where a sinner can talk with a fellow human being who shares the values of Christ.

It is difficult to enter into any conversations where basic misunderstandings recur, and one such misunderstanding centers on what "sorrow for sin" is all about. Now it is clear that when we admit that our freedom is impoverished we are not necessarily admitting guilt. There is a kind of clinical attitude towards one's past use of freedom that can be found in the crassest and most godless person. His clinical objectivity in his own regard in no way implies that he considers himself guilty or culpable. To admit guilt, one must trace the impoverishment of freedom back to the very source of oneself and see at that source the unheeding, excluding, selfish willfulness that is at work in one's actions. Furthermore, sorrow for sin means that we take one more step. We are not merely observers of our personal guilt. We are its accusers. We are not talking about feelings of guilt, however. Such feelings are all too easy to capitalize upon in the name of religion. Yet it is true that it is most difficult to describe this guilt which exists in us, partly as memory, partly as feeling, partly as admission. But to admit guilt is one thing; to be sorry for it is another.

To illustrate this problem, let us refer once again to a scene from *La Strada*. Its hero, Zampano, is caught in the cords which stretch from a cruel and insensitive past to a moment of solitude in which his former brutish manliness and vanity are reduced to scale. It is night. He is on an empty shore to which his drunken stupor has brought him. He shudders at the overarching loneliness which matches his own solitude. His eyes sweep the dark distances over the waters which are as broad and as deep as his own mute incommunicability. He weeps. Is this "sorrow for

50

sin"? Certainly it is an admission of guilt. Zampano does not attribute his misuse of freedom to circumstances, although these may have had a part, or to other people, though they played an important role. Circumstance and other people have disappeared from that lonely shore. The finger of accusation is there. But "sorrow for sin" is something more. It consists, so to speak, in the desire to reach back, to touch and to heal that past; to bring together the past with the present in such a way as to make the finger of accusation irrelevant. Or rather, to reach out for the hand that accuses in a plea for peace. "Sorrow for sin" is a desire for reconciliation with a person. But reconciliation with whom? With all those who suffered from one's misuse of freedom and from whom one is alienated. "Sorrow for sin" implies the will to restore to them and to oneself dignity and hope. That is why no one should "forgive the sins" of someone who is not "sorry for them." The Church can invite people to what the Scripture calls *metanoia*—to a new outlook on sin and integrity; it can invite them to take part in that reconciling conversation which is the sacrament of penance; but there can be no true reconciliation between man and God until man moves beyond mere admission of guilt and desires wholeness.

Yet it perhaps could be argued that the possibilities for freedom, and therefore for culpable sin, sorrow for sin, and meaningful confession, are rather limited. It is true that we must be free to sin, and this is what the Church has always meant when it speaks of "sufficient reflection" and "full consent of the will." Nevertheless the sacrament of penance is not simply a matter of discovering the degree of the misuse of freedom in oneself—a difficult task, to say the least. It is rather instituted (made into a permanent institution) to give people the opportunity to talk *about* sin.

But what is "penance"? Why does the Church ask the sinner, even after he has contritely confessed his sins, to "make up" for

51

them? Certainly, God does not need to be *personally* placated. If so, then any notion of "doing penance" for sins has to mean that one attempts to begin, so to speak, where the sin left off; that one begins to use the freedom that was misused before. If we make up for anything, it is for lost time, for a contact which we have lost, for an enrichment that is yet to come. Penances do not look back; they look ahead. The few prayers we normally say as our "penance" are symbolic of our return to a renewed Christian life. They are not symbolic of a return to "the scene of the crime" but to new solidarity with our Lord. In the sacramental conversation of penance, our sins are forgiven and forgotten with a constancy, even a stubbornness, that will have nothing to do with the past. The story of the prodigal son bears this truth out. This does not mean that we cannot learn from the past. In earlier times, in fact, penances were more directly educational. They centered on aspects of human life which tend to be the most vulnerable to the selfishness that is at the root of sin. Thus sex, food, and sleep all promise the prolongation of the life of the individual and thereby demonstrate his importance. These three things became the matter of penances in order to show that the individual's importance did not override all other persons who happened to cross his path. This is, no doubt, a hard lesson to learn. But the sacramental conversation should be such that the penitent approaches his lesson in a confident mood. Any attitude towards penances which does not embody and convey this confidence does not belong to the sacrament of penance.

We wish also to examine in this chapter the matter of confessional "judgment." Our purpose will be to assess the nature and scope of the "absolution" which is given in confession, and the role of the person who hears the confession. The priest's role is often described as that of a judge who, upon hearing the evidence presented by the penitent, comes to a verdict which, in most cases, is an authoritative absolution of the penitent. If confession, like conversation, is a dying art, it is in large measure due to the confusion which results from describing it in terms that are easily capable of misunderstanding. One such description is that which likens the sacrament of penance to a judicial process. The scriptural background for this idea of judicial process is the biblical notion of judgment. What insights do the scriptural data give us?

One reason we must be cautious in this matter is that the New Testament seems to give the impression that judgment is something that comes only at the end of life. Hence when the idea of judgment is applied to the sacrament of penance, we are forced to consider the absolution merely as forestalling a future condemnation or as insuring a future favorable judgment. This view, of course, would deprive the sacrament of its secular meaning.

Even when we overcome that hurdle and view the judgment passed on the sinner in his life as a participation in, and not merely a preparation for, a final judgment, we manage to get ourselves into the wrong frame of mind. We are too vividly aware of the menacing aspects of final judgment. We forget, first of all, that damnation is reserved for the unrepentant and not for penitents. The imagery of the judgment of God is drawn heavily from Old Testament representations of the Day of Yahweh and of the wrath of that day. The wrath, of course, is directed against those who do not know (that is, love) God and who do not obey the Gospel (2 Thess. 1, 8). "God has not destined us for wrath," says Paul, "but to obtain salvation through Our Lord Jesus Christ, who died for us so that whether we wake or sleep (whether in this life or the next) we might live with him. Therefore encourage one another and build one another up, just as you are doing" (1 Thess. 5, 9–11). Texts like the preceding one indicate that it is certainly not the wrathful judgment that the sacrament of penance is imitating, since the act of a Christian who confesses his sins is already a sign that he is beyond the severe judgment of God.

Second, we forget that "menace" is used metaphorically and not literally of God. Despite all the imagery which makes God's judgment seem vindictive and threatening, in itself that judgment can only be a work of love. That is why Dante could use as his superscription for the entrance into hell the well-known words "Eternal love made me."

There is some paradox here but we should not invoke paradox too quickly in explaining how "God's judgment" is exercised in the sacrament of penance. For one thing, the New Testament terminology which describes Christ's ministry of forgiveness stands, as it were, on its own and apart from the New Testament terminology which speaks of judgment. We look in vain for one passage where the two terminologies join. Again, Christ uses the term "judgment" as a synonym for mercy, for faith, and for charity (Mt. 12, 18, 20; 23, 23; Lk. 11, 42). As practiced by Christ's followers judgment is to be a creative restoring action. Judgment in the sense of harsh, condemnatory judgment is precisely to be avoided (Mt. 7, 12). It is the creative sense of judgment that is exercised in the sacrament of penance. To describe the sacrament as a judicial process is to place the sacrament outside the context of charity and into a context of perfect societies, officials, and so forth. We need to restore, with the help of the scriptural data, a sane perspective to this matter of judgment, of sin.

The scriptural data can be difficult to deal with, however. We have seen how the imagery of the day of wrath can confuse the issue. Yet St. John's theology of judgment, if we have the patience to work through some initial confusion, offers us a view of judgment that is much more appropriate to the sacrament which we are considering. The initial confusion stems from the fact

54

that, in John's presentation, (a) Christ is *not* a judge (3, 17; 12, 47); (b) Christ *is* a judge (5, 22, 27; 8, 26); (c) the Father is not a judge (5, 22; 8, 50); (d) both the Father and the Son judge (8, 16). How to interpret these conflicting statements? It seems that the negative statements imply that the kind of judgment which Christ reveals is *new* by any existing standards. It is new first of all in that it is not a judgment which is passed on man consequent upon his actions. Judgment is already at work in the actions of man (3, 18–19; 16, 8–11). Second, the way in which judgment is at work is that one truth-bearing person, Christ, confronts man and by the very claim that he lays to the truth invites man to accept him. In John's theology, this confrontation is the judgment in its basic sense. It has a negative aspect, it is true: judgment describes man's unwillingness to accept the person, the word, the name of Christ (3, 18–19; 12, 48). In that unwillingness judgment is already passed on man. Man is condemned to remain in darkness, which is to say that he has not accepted the positive, upbuilding kind of judgment which God freely wishes to pass on man but cannot do so without man's cooperation. But this unwillingness is not a judgment passed by God or by Christ. It is man's own personal statement made in his own regard. Any language which seems to imply a negative statement passed by God on man is therefore figurative. This is borne out by John when he attributes to the Spirit the role of convincing man that evil is not the inevitable, domineering necessity in human life which it claims to be (16, 8–11). The judgment confrontation, as John describes it, is best captured in the following text (3, 16–21):

> For God so loved the world that he gave his only Son, that whoever believes in him should not perish but have eternal life. For God sent the Son into the world, not to condemn the world, but that the world might be saved through him. He who believes in him is not condemned; he who does not believe is condemned

55

already, because he has not believed in the name of the only Son of God. And this is the judgment, that the light has come into the world, and men loved the darkness rather than light, because their deeds were evil. For every one who does evil hates the light, and does not come to the light, lest his deeds should be exposed. But he who does what is true comes to the light, that it may be clearly seen that his deeds have been wrought in God.

Thus the newness of judgment in John's theology consists in the realization that God is present to men as their ally against the debilitating experience of evil; that his presence is experienced in the person of Christ; that man in his freedom can refuse the support of God and thereby fall prey to a self-judgment which, more than anything else, embodies threat and menace to his human existence.

Does the sacrament of penance involve a similar confrontation as the one we have just been describing? We cannot draw an exact parallel because, as we have said earlier, the sinner who comes to the sacrament is already, by the very fact that he does come more than a sinner in John's sense. But insofar as someone comes to the sacrament of penance seeking, in faith, a favorable judgment from God, he should expect to find himself not in the presence of threat, but in the presence of a God who is already committed to him in Christ.

We have tried to show that we can go wide of the mark theologically, not to mention psychologically, if we are not careful to understand aright the notions of sin and judgment that are usually associated with the sacrament of penance. A further consideration of these same two notions is now necessary in order to get a more rounded picture of the kind of conversation which is envisaged in this sacrament.

Our sins, as we have said, our personal sins, perhaps even our private sins, by reason of the normal processes by which freedoms interact, hurt other people. They deprive others of that witness to the victorious charity of Christ which they need if they are to grow in that charity themselves. To observe violence or hatred, or to be their victim, cuts into our limited supply of faith and hope, and makes us, even if we do not wish to strike back, cynical about life and about its potentialities. When others see our violence and hatred, they are affected in the same way. Sin, therefore, sets up community vibrations. It contributes to a moral atmosphere which can be as amorphous and choking as any physical atmosphere. The confession of "my" sin to "the person" whom I have offended would be sufficient were it the case that I and this person existed in some moral vacuum apart from other men. But such is not the case. Moreover, we must ask whether or not people need the opportunity to express at least symbolically their consciousness of the communal nature of sin. This awareness is part of our human concern, and it calls for some forum in which we can express it. Confession made to a community figure is certainly one way in which our concern and sorrow can be voiced.

As far as judgment is concerned, it too has a communal aspect. We have not yet given sufficient attention to the fact that *all* are called to share in the creative judgment of God on the individual sinner. This judgment centers, it is true, in the priest's absolution, but the priest is acting in this case as a public person in the community. The judgment he makes is his own, but "his own" here is no more to be taken in some absolutely isolated sense than is the judgment which Christ passes on sinners. Rather, just as Christ wishes his whole Church to share in his kind of judgment on sin, so the absolution of the priest calls for the community's involvement in the absolution. To say, as Trent did say, that the priest is the "sole minister" of this sacrament does not mean that he is the only one concerned. He is, so to speak, the sole minister of the Church's concern. And even his function of being sole minister is, as we will try to show in another chapter, intended to focus for the community its own living

57

out the words and actions of Christ. If we come to realize both
the communal aspect of sin and the communal aspect of judgment or absolution, we will find it easier to understand why so
much attention has been given in recent times to the theology
of penance as a reconciliation with the Church. However, this
latter terminology, while it does not obscure the secular form
of this sacrament (because this sacrament deals with conversation about the human dimensions of Christian living), does
obscure its secular aim. By this we mean that the terminology
"reconciliation with the Church" does not make the point sufficiently clear that Christ's desire is to reconcile the world to
himself *through* the Church. Penance therefore is properly speaking a step towards reconciliation with the world, insofar as
Christ has made this world his own in the Church. The sacrament is at the same time an activity within the world which
faces up to the personal and communal sin in the world, and a
sign to the world that a community exists in its midst which calls
for reconciliation and forgiveness across all national, cultural,
and personal lines. The absolution of the sinner by the priest
carries with it the presumption of a community concern for the
sinner, and a promise that there are people in his life—in the
life of the world—who want to forgive and forget, whose total
attitude is to try to imitate the constructive judgment of God on
sin. The priest should, insofar as he is a confessor, try to communicate this realization to the penitent. His own attitude and
conduct in the confessional will probably go farthest in doing
this task. As a preacher, moreover, he has the opportunity to
underscore this community aspect of sin and of absolution, and
to speak of the serious commission this sacrament puts on Christians to look upon the absolution of the sinner not only as his
gesture but as their sacramental gesture and, in hope, the world's
as well.

58

4.

An Agreement to Love

Love has a point at which nothing can be said, demanded, denied, or even done. One simply loves. This point of love is private and intimate because it involves the inclination of one's inmost and most inclusive self towards another person. Such a point of love resists our categories and tends to make commentary banal. It defines itself only in terms of itself, or so at least the poets and the saints tell us. Ethicians, on the other hand (like mathematicians), tell us that a point has no extension. So they inquire instead about coordinates of time, of place, of hypothetical circumstance—things that seem to blur the simplicity of love's central inclination.

Is the point of love, as moralists sometimes seem to insinuate, an impersonal conceptual summation of what are in fact discrete, prosaic experiences of providing, encouraging, giving pleasure, conversing, planning—each with its own separate rules? Is love an abstraction—a quiet place in the mind where two people pause and try to measure how far they have come and with what forces they can move on? Does Christian theology discuss marriage too exclusively in terms of the space-time circumstances of love, neglecting the point of love itself? Does the sacrament of marriage presuppose this point of love or does it bring it about? Is sacramental marriage really just a social concession but otherwise without any direct and humanly significant contribution to the married love of the couple? In other words, what

59

difference does receiving this sacrament make and where is its effectiveness to be observed? Does Christ's engagement in the sacramental union coincide precisely with the promise of love made by the partners, or does he in some sense intrude upon and correct the vows they pronounce? If baptism radically introduces us into the Christian life, why are so many other conditions and circumstances attached to marriage before it can arrive at that lofty point where it becomes a "valid Christian marriage"? In short, what recognizable and profoundly human activity does the sacrament of marriage embody? We approach these questions all too often from the standpoint of the natural law. Much of what Catholics say about married love is put forward under the rubric of natural law. This is an unfortunate situation because the expression "natural law" is used differently by different groups at the present time. As the normal non-believer uses the expression, it means what reasonable men can *de facto* agree upon, readily and with conviction, when they examine the ideal and concrete circumstance of moral action. When, on the other hand, the Catholic Church speaks about natural law, there is a subtle shift of emphasis away from the question of the *content* of the law to the question of the *source of our knowledge* of that content. The Church says in effect (1) that if there were such things as reasonable men, they would readily and with conviction arrive at the same conclusions as she does in those moral matters where she bases her teaching on natural law; but (2) men are not reasonable in the above sense because, without some acceptance of revelation, they cannot *de facto* reach those same conclusions. Thus, the Church's actual use of the expression "natural law" is made in the context of a revelation on which the Church must reflect before it can make its statements about man. Natural law, then, is a theological locus, that is, it is one of the ways in which Christians attempt to understand and to express a more inclusive faith-experience. We do not mean to say that the Church cannot talk about the nature of marriage with men of all beliefs. The Church should not be expected to stay away from the questions which concern men in all their naturalness. But the Church has a different global inspiration for its moral judgments, and the main source of these judgments is God's revelation. Once this becomes clear, Catholics will be better able to discuss marriage with secular humanists and fellow Christians. No one in the discussion is without presuppositions, and unless these presuppositions are brought out into the open, we all risk being reduced to accepting *whatever happens* in marriage as our ideal of marriage. For Christians, this kind of happening-theology is a denial of an historical, biblical revelation concerning marriage. Such a revelation does in fact exist, and it will be the basis for our theological interpretation of the sacrament of marriage as the choosing of a specific standard against which human love is to be measured.

The first thing we see as we look at this sacrament is that, unlike the others, it is not a gesture which is made by the Christian community. At least it is not made by a public person in the community. The couple themselves are not acting *solely* as the representatives of the community's convictions about married love. Hence we have had in the past, sacramental marriages without the witnesses required by present Church legislation; and today we have sacramental marriages (those between Catholics and non-Christians) where at least one minister of the sacrament may be presumed not to share the community's convictions about married love. What conclusions should we draw from this? It certainly does not follow that there is no meaningful relation between the sacramental union and the presence of the Church's witnesses. The latter might be required by the former as a reasonable consequence of the meaning of sacrament. But in the sacramental action, there is the more observable fact that two people are making all kinds of promises to each other about life together and, in some as yet undefined sense, in Christ. We will

61

begin our analysis, then, with what is, or should be, going on in the minds and hearts of the Christian parties to a sacramental marriage.

A description of the marriage vows that has too often been carelessly given is that they constitute a *contractual consent.* Thus one of the major criticisms levelled against Catholic teaching on marriage is that it is too legalistic in its outlook. The idea of a legal contract seemed to dominate everything about Catholic marriage. Yet the legal and lawful aspects of marriage are not unimportant. Legal contracts have, after all, a great deal to say about the human condition. One can even be lyrical, as Plato was, on how their formulation and implementation relieve man of a certain basic rudeness and inclination towards hostility. A contract, too, can stand for a man's word, on which to an extent his honor stands. So we ought not be overcritical of legal contracts, or say that the idea of marriage as a legal contract is necessarily a dehumanized one. This is so even if the notion of contract seems at times to minimize or obscure the qualities of affectivity and interpersonal giving which we associate with marriage.

The central paragraph in the marital contract, and to many people its most demeaning article, is that which gives to each partner a right over the other's body. Though this traditional understanding of marriage has often been caricatured, its primary insight is to show that marriage is an exchange of *rights,* not of bodies. In this same tradition, one's rights are the tokens of one's individuality and dignity. To give a right over to another is to make the other a part of oneself, a part of all the personal striving that is envisaged in life. It means that henceforth one person finds his radical dignity only in the other. That one person is fulfilled (or "practices perfection," as an earlier terminology had it) only in fulfilling another. To place all one's honor and all one's dignity henceforth in another fragile and free human person is no small ideal. There is more humanity in it than in unions which are motivated by calculation, by planned self-interest, or by conspiracy to keep-others-out. Despite all this, what remained in people's minds as "Church teaching" was often and unfortunately the isolated matter of rendering a physical debt which was legally and religiously ratified in the sacrament of marriage.

The notion of a legal contract thus seemed to fail to give an adequate picture of the Church's teaching on marriage. Perhaps this misunderstanding was due to the fact that the proper Christian setting or context for any such talk about a contract had been lost or ignored. That setting is essentially one which God reveals to men in Christ; it is not any natural law which provides the primary inspiration for the Church's teaching. The proper Christian context is that of the *covenant*, the pact made with man by God and with God by man.

The covenant is a complex reality. It includes both the relationship of Yahweh to Israel in the Old Testament, and the new covenant between Christ and his people. It is therefore an historical reality. It develops in several stages. It is communal, in the sense that it makes community by drawing the individual into the wider community of God and his fellow men. The particular phases and the detail of this covenant are too complex to describe here. Yet from the beginning of salvation history to its high point in Christ's love for the Church (Eph. 5, 23), there is an identifiable pattern of attitudes, a continuing stance of interpersonal relationships. This pattern becomes the paradigm for Christian marriage. In recent years, many theologians have pointed out that the covenant had a secularizing effect on such things as politics, religion, and law. The further point which needs to be made is that it had a secularizing effect on our understanding of marriage as well. That is, *by becoming itself the model for Christian marriage, the covenant makes that marriage like itself:* a total encounter in which man's integrity and development are at stake at every step; a partnership in which love, fidelity, anger, curiosity, sloth, protestations, stubbornness, passionate pursuit, renewed effort, anguish, recrimination, tranquility, and tenderness are all a part.

The diversity of secular attitudes just listed is, however, contained within a certain unity. The same covenant continues to bind; its God and Lord is single-minded, faithful, even jealous. The passion which the covenant provokes makes sense only if we suppose that the covenant envisages an enduring, intensely personal relationship between the parties to it. And if we are to take the covenant seriously as the standard, the model which sets the ideal dimensions of Christian married love, it is hardly an exaggeration to conclude that Christian marriage is exclusive and permanent.

It is the covenant-model, then, which provides the basic inspiration for the permanent and exclusive style of Christian marriage. We have here a wider and deeper basis for that style than any consideration of "the good of the children" could provide. The covenant is also a model which indicates the secularity of sacramental marriage, by making that marriage the meeting place of intensified emotion, of expanded trust, and of deepened resolution.

Now it is obvious that the covenant begins with God and stems from his initiative. The faults and limitations of man, in his part of the deal, are equally obvious. Christians are affirming, in the sacramental action, that man is subject to God's initiative if man is to attain to a secularity in married love that is not marred by idolatry, legalism, hardness of heart, or a failure of trust. Christian marriage vows, therefore, are not so private to the parties concerned that the parties can rely on their own ingenuity and sufficiency either to determine the ideal of marriage or to carry it out. The vows are at once promise and prayer; they are an acceptance of a certain intrusion, so to speak, on the part of God. They leave room for the insights of God in the formulation of what human life and love are all about; they welcome God's continuing presence in the living-out of married love.

Moreover, the Christian believes that the insights and presence of God are mediated through Christ's Church. Now this mediation, like the Incarnation itself, takes place in history and culture, in science and art, above all in *people,* especially in people who believe in Christ. Therefore, the Christian sacrament of marriage inevitably opens up those who receive it to a broader secular perspective than they ordinarily would associate with marriage. The sacramental gesture has a social dimension. Concretely, for the Christian, one cannot love in this life—not even that seemingly intimate love we find in marriage—without the Christian community. This is hardly an astounding statement, providing one seriously accepts the covenant-model outlined above. Without a community which espouses the same ideal of covenant love, it is hard to see how any married couple could keep striving for that ideal for very long.

This latter consideration perhaps explains why the community's witnesses have an important role in the sacrament of marriage. They are there to symbolize the inherent relationship between the partners and Christ's community in the effective pursuit of married love by partners. They are witnesses to the partners' acceptance of covenant-love as the standard of married love. They are there to pledge the community's support to the couple as they attempt to embody the covenant-love in their lives.

However, the partners *are* the ministers of this sacrament. Everything hinges on their initial, free determination to take upon themselves the standard of covenant-love as the pattern for their lives together. Here their privacy and their solitary judgment are uppermost. That this judgment should be made

65

by Christians hardly offends the conscience of anyone who has accepted in faith that revelation of which covenant-love as the model of human married love is a part! If someone has not accepted that revelation as the basic inspiration for his conscientious action, then marrying "in the Church" makes no sense. What we cannot say is that the mere action of trading marriage vows in a church building automatically, by reason of some sacramental mechanism, creates in the partners the mentality whereby covenant-love becomes their standard of married life. Rather, accepting that standard is part of the sacramental action itself, so that where this acceptance is lacking (at least in the Christian partner) there is no sacrament.

We are discussing here a very delicate and complicated matter. For what sort of *formal acceptance* of covenant-love as the model for human love is required before a sacramental marriage occurs? This question becomes particularly acute when we realize, as was already indicated, that the dimensions of covenant-love are themselves developing and being discovered as the historically rooted Christian community gains insight into the revelation of God concerning marriage.

What traditionally has been required as the intention of the minister of any sacrament in the Church is that he "do what the Church does." This is admittedly a vague kind of intention, yet vagueness of motive is often the normal and not the exceptional kind of human volition. Perhaps only fanatics are able to reduce human motivation to the sharp contours of clearly separate acts, each tagged with its appropriate label and moral valence. At any rate, we may apply this same notion of intention to the matter of sacramental marriage. Hence to determine theologically whether and when a sacramental marriage occurs, we must ask whether or not the partners intend to do what the Church does in the area of marriage.

Perhaps we have been overhasty in the past to answer this

66

question in the affirmative. By this we do not mean that sacramental marriages (that is, marriages in which the partners choose, at least implicitly, the covenant-love model) occur rarely; though on the other hand they may not occur as frequently as we might think. This last observation is made as a theological assessment of sacramental marriage. It is not made as a reaction against the intricate processes involved in gathering evidence, in annulment cases, concerning the initial marriage intention. Such processes have been the subject of much complaint; yet the question of evidence is, and ought to remain, distinct from the question of the nature of intention in sacramental marriage. The theological task is to provide a sufficiently intelligible picture of sacramental marriage so that, when the question of validity is raised, an equally intelligible answer can be given to it. Thus it is necessary to ask here whether, in an area as private to the marriage partners as their mutual human love, a decision is obviously present to make Christ, through his community, a judge, a molder, a voice, a commentator, an influential factor in that human love. We must also discover what psychological and social factors are present in the marriage intentions of two people today. In any case, we may not easily presuppose that sufficient formal or informal acceptance of covenant-love standard is present in Church marriages, for in the sacramental decision to let Christ enter into the center of human love people go far beyond the point of what is "socially acceptable."

In mixed marriages, however, one party radically accepts covenant-love as the standard of married love, and the other party often does not. In what way can such a marriage be sacramental? If the covenant sets a secular standard for married love, we must honestly admit that, in mixed marriages, we are not dealing simply with different "allegiances" or "denominations." Basic issues of life and love are involved. Where different faiths are involved, there is a strain placed on dating, courtship, the

67

marriage ceremony and married life itself. The beginnings of a theology of such mixed marriages can be found in the observation that the non-believing partner, in accepting the Christian partner, has already in some real sense accepted the covenant-love model which presumably has taken root in and fused with the deepest personality of the beloved one. Moreover, we must remember that the kind of love which we call covenant-love, exists in individuals outside the Christian community. Where, however, there is a radical difference of standard between the partners of a mixed marriage, their union remains humanly hazardous. To associate all the hazard with the question of the religious education of potential children is simply to avoid the real issue.

In his work *Marriage: Human Reality and Saving Mystery,* Edward Schillebeeckx has demonstrated how the Old Testament and New Testament revelation of the covenant is expressed in language taken *from* human married love; and that revelation in turn becomes the standard *for* human married love. This would seem to be either a contradiction or mere tautology (human married love is the standard for human married love). However, we must keep in mind the fact that the language of marriage (or any language), when it is employed to describe the revelation of God in history, acquires new meanings determined by the total context of that revelation. Hence when the same language reappears again to describe Christian marriage in itself, it reappears carrying the new meanings it has acquired in the context of revelation. Thus it is that the ideal dimensions of married love can be expanded or sharpened by Christian revelation, without the vocabulary of love changing very much at all.

Schillebeeckx also has shown that the New Testament revelation about marriage points, in a real sense, beyond marriage. It does so by its counsel of virginity. But does not this counsel conflict with our thesis that Christianity has reinforced the secular nature of marriage?

We cannot escape this problem simply by stating that there is no logical contradiction between affirming the secularity of marriage on the one hand, and on the other saying that there is more to Christianity than secular married love. That "more" is bothersome. We are dealing here with a mood that almost defies logic. If, in Schillebeeckx's words, Christ has put marriage "in its place" and has relativized the value of marriage, have we not found ourselves in a Church where sacramental marriage will be constantly overshadowed by "higher" values that are foreign to the secular lives that married people are trying to live in Christ? Are we not saying that some Christians are experiencing something that is more than secular? And does this not imply that a married, secular Christianity is less than some other, better kind of Christianity?

We cannot simply say that the purpose of virginity is to *call attention* to Christ. Not to Christ as one who relativizes the secular, nor to Christ as one who has something to say about marriage, but simply to Christ whose personal attractiveness and importance to men are such that we think it urgent to draw attention to him by means of the gesture of virginity (which is one of the best attention-getters of all time). The virtue of such an explanation would be that it would make virginity less offensive to Christian married couples, because it would assign as the motive for virginity not a rejection of the secular but rather a valid desire to center the Christian's concern on Christ. But it does not fully resolve the difficulty which the Christian tradition on virginity presents.

This tradition has viewed the sign of virginity as one which deals with a conflict of loves, with priorities in love. The sign of virginity does have built into it a challenge, even a protest; it affirms that the love of God in Christ is more precious than the deepest, purest, richest love (married or otherwise) which excludes God. Rather, it wishes to extend to that love the possibilities of enriching itself even more; and in the expression "even more" we *do* attach to virginity a specificity which does relativize married love. The question now becomes: *whose* married love? For it is always important to find out who is making a sign to whom. We suggest that virginity is not a sign made by celibate Christians to non-celibate Christians. It is not made by one group in the Church to another. It is made rather by the Church to the world. It does not, therefore, relativize Christian married love, as Schillebeeckx suggests, for it is not talking to Christian married couples. Virginity as practiced by some members in the Church is addressed to those who do not open themselves up to a religious dimension in their married love. But this means that virginity is unworldly, even anti-worldly; it does not mean that it is anti-marriage. On the contrary, by the sign of virginity the Church wishes to introduce Christ into the married lives and loves of all men and women. But Christian married couples, by their very reception of the sacrament of marriage, have *already accepted* the challenge which Christ presents to married love. They should not, therefore, unless they are worldly, be disturbed by the fact that some members in the Church are undertaking virginity in order to affirm something that married people, by the reception of the sacrament of marriage, have themselves affirmed, namely, that Christ is a part of their human love.

5.
The Delegation

In our lives, we keep meeting death. We read about it in headlines and essays, in memoirs and forecasts. Some deaths seem to stand out: the ovens, the deranged finale of Hitler, the pyres of Ghandi or Nehru reflecting the distorted grief of India, the drawn-out departures of Churchill or Pope John, the young victims of political violence in our own country. And other deaths closer to home: someone who has been a part of our life and of its fragile meaning, a half-made child, and sometimes, just a name vaguely remembered.

It is difficult for us to encompass the shame and disintegration of death. So, we disguise it in our language where euphemism replaces a frank admission of the fact of death. In our parlors of death, we make the intractable and bloodless flesh express for the last time some faint and optimistic human sentiment. We even push away the thought of death, simply because we do not know what to think of it. Death seems to be the ultimate insult. Our time-and-space existence calls for some benediction that will fill out and fulfill the pattern of thought and activities that we have begun. Instead, it seems to be cursed. "The world was made for the dead," says one of Flannery O'Connor's characters. "There's a million times more dead than living and the dead are dead a million times longer than the living are alive."

Christians have in many ways been prolific on the subject of

71

death, however. We meet in Christian liturgy and literature the constant protestation that death is not the evil thing that the world has made it seem. We find treatises on the Art of Dying Well; rules for religious who are about to die; prayers for assorted classes of dead people in the singular and plural; long-term and short-term remembrances of the dead; disputes over the proper way to dispose of dead bodies; episcopal decisions concerning the relative pomp advisable or allowable during the last journey; private devotions whereby the fulfilling of precisely set-down conditions insures the grace of a good death.

What is this "good death" that is so central to the Church's sacrament of anointing? Can we even discuss the matter without seeming to be haggling over the grave? We must, if the secular city is made up not only of Pretty Young People for whom the subject of death is understandably remote, but also of some pretty old people who understandably ask what is around the corner at the end of the street.

We must begin our discussion by saying that the fine distinctions drawn between sickness and dying in many theologies of the last anointing are perhaps too fine. On this point there is some fluidity in the Church's teaching language. St. Thomas, whose point of view was adopted both at Florence and at Trent, did not hesitate to call the last anointing "the sacrament of those on their way out" (*sacramentum exeuntium: Suppl.*, q. 32, a. 1). It is true that this language neglects an earlier terminology which spoke of "the sacrament of the sick," but the reasons are obvious. When one examines the earlier tradition, much of it appears to have understood by "the sick" people who were gravely ill and not simply victims of the common cold. Moreover, the state of medical science being what it was, every sickness might well have been final. At any rate, in what follows we intend to speak of the dying and the seriously sick interchangeably. Most Christians

72

seem to agree that this sacrament addresses itself to those situations of human existence which are critical precisely because they place men in a position of grave physical and spiritual weakness and ineptitude (see *Suppl.*, q. 30, a. 1). The meaning of "physical weakness and ineptitude" is clear; "spiritual weakness and ineptitude" calls for some further remarks.

The latter expression probably means something different to people for whom "the spiritual" itself has different meanings. If one disassociates "the spiritual" from the normal psychological processes of fear, self-doubt, remorse, resentment, then it would be indeed difficult to see how "spiritual weakness and ineptitude" could become a burning, relevant issue at the prospect of death. If, on the other hand, the expression "the spiritual" provides no means of escape for human experience, if it forces us to a greater penetration of that human experience, then the human style and reality of our weakness and ineptitude at the prospect of death become evident. As St. Thomas says, this weakness takes place "in the mind itself" (*in ipsa mente: Suppl.*, q. 30, a. 1).

It is not merely a question of our being psychologically defenseless in the face of death; nor merely a question of a certain clumsiness that weighs upon someone who faces an unknown after-life. We are talking here more specifically of a weakness and ineptitude which relates to one's very secular Christian belief and hope and living. A Christian lifespan will normally have included a great deal of undigested beliefs, unprincipled superstitions, a tenuous grasp of God's providence in one's own regard let alone in regard to the lives of those we have loved or hated or hurt, a gravitation towards Christ which was as halting as it was sure. The discrepancy between a high but necessarily obscure ideal and a vividly low performance level crowds in at critical moments such as we are discussing here. The realization of this discrepancy can tear at the sick person, can humiliate him and overwhelm him. In effect, it may tempt him to *negate radically the value of his human life* and to regret having lived that life in Christ's communion.

We suggest that what we are dealing with in the last anointing is a symbolic gesture on the part of the Christian community of support and of prayer for the sick person. The prayer-form of the words said during the anointing is not without its own symbolism: it expresses a certain assessment of the situation as being pretty much out of the hands of all present and hence as being particularly in need of an intervention of God. But it is rather about the *support* found in the anointing that we wish to speak. The anointing itself is supposed to imitate a medical healing, such as putting balm on wounds. However, *the medical gesture cannot be taken out of its context*. In respect to its context the last anointing most resembles *a delegation of concerned and sympathetic fellow Christians* whose presence and prayers are intended to be of meaningful assistance to the person in his weakness and ineptitude. The anointing has a quality about it that we might best describe as a "holding action." St. Thomas remarks that no new Christian tasks fall to the sick person by reason of the anointing; it is "solely" a question "of a remedy" (*Suppl.*, q. 30, a. 2). But what sort of remedy?

Because the last anointing is a sacrament, this does not mean that we may neglect the insight which will identify it as a humanly intelligible and meaningful activity. We are all familiar with delegations to the sick and dying. We know their utility and their shortcomings. We sense their nervous entrance, yet the bold face they put on. We see that their strained but determined good will gets through to the sick person. It cuts into his loneliness, painfully but surely. The delegation helps him set his Christian life in perspective; it demonstrates to him that he is one with Christians who are capable after all of only small gestures of love and hope, but who nevertheless are convinced that Christ is the Lord of life beyond this life and in all its stages. The sick person is made one with the Church in its perilous faith, in its affirmation of life in the face of death, in its pride in a providential thread that can, artfully and with grace, knit together sorry patches of a past which has left many frightening memories in its wake. Christ is the Lord over dead memories as well as over the shadowy corners of the human psyche. His healing makes whole; it achieves what each man wishes, what each man fails to do, namely, to be able *to sum it all up* and say "it was good." This is the main message of the delegation. In the last anointing there is a return to the first creation. It is this sense that justifies tradition calling the last anointing "a preparation for glory."

There are two factors which militate against the above understanding of the sacrament of anointing. The first is a failure to understand the anointing as a *community* action. It is necessary to insist on the communal nature of the last anointing. St. Thomas speaks of the priest who administers this sacrament as a "public person." In this sense the priest inevitably represents the wishes and convictions of the community of Christ. No doubt, with this sacrament as with the rest of the Church's reality, many people would prefer to deal directly with Christ (usually viewed more as divine than as human), forgetting the community of persons in which we actually encounter him. The irony here is that once more we miss the point of the Incarnation; we fail to bask in those human gestures in which God's favor is *de facto* mediated. The man who does not experience the humanity of the Church's gestures in the sacraments runs the risk of never seeing salvation as having anything to do with his own humanity, personal or social. Not only would the sick person be thereby deprived of the human consolation and solidarity so needed in his crisis, but the community itself would become blind to its own responsibility towards individuals who are sick.

75

It would become callous towards the real dimensions of the sick person's struggle to assess his past. In this it may deprive itself of the ability to assess its own past as well.

The second factor is that the sacrament of anointing seems to be administered in very suspicious circumstances, for example after death, or during an unfortunate accident, or under an oxygen tent. In these cases there is little indication that the sick person is receiving a consoling delegation from the Church. Indeed, a delegation in these circumstances seems an intrusion. Yet what seems uppermost is to get that oil applied to that forehead while there still might be breath left in the body. Two considerations may be useful here. First, the above situations are the exceptional ones, not the normal ones. We cannot take them as offering the best example of what the Church is trying to do in this sacrament, nor the chief source for our understanding this sacrament. In the normal situation, as we have described it earlier, the sick person is relatively conscious and therefore susceptible to the anxieties we have mentioned.

Second, much of the fanaticism connected with this sacrament is activated by the desire to insure that the sins of the dying person be forgiven. Indeed, this result is attributed to the sacrament in Christian belief. We often hear it said that the dying person has "squared things with God." But often this statement implies that God has become progressively angrier with our lives and that he lays aside this anger only when the last anointing takes place. But is not the problem that *we* might have become progressively or accumulatively angry with our lives? That *we* risk spitting out our past accomplishments, our hopes along with our failures, like so many cold ashes? That *we* might despair of any crown or blessing for our humanity? These problems call for a delegation of sympathetic Christians. Where, then, does the "forgiveness of sins" fit in?

For one thing, it is important to recall that we should at most look upon the forgiveness of sins as a by-product of this sacrament, and not as its main point. St. Thomas offers a shrewd analysis here. He says, in effect, that if a man is willing to receive the kind of gracious gesture of the Christian community that we have in the last anointing, then that willingness is incompatible with sin. Now this is a comment (almost an obvious one) on the *psychological* situation of the sick person. One need not deny that both the community's gesture and the individual's willingness to accept it are gifts (graces) of God. But on the other hand one need not so stress this point that we miss understanding, in human terms, what is going on. A man's willingness to have Christ, through his Church, speak to the totality of his human life is a sign of an abundant trust. Where that trust exists there is already salvation, there is capacity to see God in one's total life and in the life of all.

But what if the willingness is present but the sacrament is not actually administered? Is there no forgiveness of sins? This would hardly follow. The actual administration of the sacrament has its obvious symbolism (it embodies the community's concern here and now for the sick person) and its proper effectiveness. But this effectiveness is not, as we have said, directly concerned with the forgiveness of sins. Moreover, we might ask why, if it is a willingness to benefit from the Church's concern and support in judging the totality of one's Christian life that creates the incompatibility with sin, we cannot presume that the incompatibility exists even where the sacrament is not actually administered. It is true that Christ has not, according to Catholic belief, *formally* guaranteed his presence save in the gestures of the Church we call sacraments. But this does not mean he is not present, in such wise that where no sacrament is actually administered there is no forgiveness of sins. The exaggeration connected with administering the last anointing no doubt stems in part from the desire of friends and relatives who are involved to be certain (with the subjective peace such certitude brings) that the sick person's sins are forgiven. Yet we should remember that our function in this sacrament is to support the sick person and not to have our own uncertainties alleviated. Moreover, in order to be certain of what we wish to be certain, we would really have to know how willing the sick person was to receive the sacrament; and this can never be known.

Our point here is not to neglect the administration of the sacrament whose virtues as a support to the dying person are clear. It is rather to minimize certain excesses in its administration which, in the long run, tend to reinforce the image of the sacraments as magic and to distract from an appreciation of their significance to real men in a real world.

One final remark is in order on this subject of the last anointing. For some people the consolation of the Christian community comes too little or too late. Such persons have an excellent instance of their human abandonment and lack of solidarity in Christ himself, dying amidst scorn and brutal indifference. It is a measure of his sensitivity that what he himself did not have he provides for others in his community and promises to be with them. That this consolation should come to the sick and dying at all is a proud boast and a humble commission of the Church as a whole. A Christian today is *against* people dying alone and unloved; he makes the last anointing a sign of his secular concern.

6.
A Simple Reminder

Who is a priest? What function does he serve in the secular city? As the answer to the first question will help us answer the second, it is necessary to inquire into the central intention of Christ in giving his Church a priesthood. No doubt, Christ's desire to continue his own priesthood figures highly in determining this central intention. Priests are living instruments of his priesthood. But as we have suggested in the case of the other sacraments, it is all too easy to forget that Christ takes concrete activities which *already* signify something truly human, and subsumes, incorporates, and fulfills this secular signification in his sacramental gestures. What human value, then, is affirmed in the institution of the priesthood? Is it merely an organizational value, a hardnosed acceptance of the fact that some few men must lead, or speak for, or tidy up after others if the job is to be done really well? Or is Christ respecting personality traits which inevitably show up only in certain individuals, by giving such individuals scope for the exercise of their highly personal endowments in the priesthood? Or does the existence of the priesthood insure the unfolding of the whole community's personality on levels far deeper than the organizational?

Even before the Christian priesthood, it was not clear to everyone that men needed priests. One Roman sage said that he could not see how two priests could pass each other on the street without bursting out laughing. We have come a long way from poking about entrails and such, but priests still seem to many people to form a vast system whose psychological supports are fear and superstition, and whose questionable premise seems to be that some men can be a crutch or substitute for other men's failings. It goes without saying that many priests today are going through a difficult period of self-questioning. We are in sore need of a realistic understanding of our Christian priesthood.

It would be well, therefore, before we begin the examination of what a priest is, to examine more closely the contemporary self-questioning that is going on among priests. According to the press, the priest's problems are celibacy, thick-thinking bishops, structural rigidity, a massive involvement in work that would better be done by laymen if done at all, and a tender yearning for the efficient freedoms of technopolitan man. For many priests, however, the problems are somewhat different; they might just even include the press at times.

Many priests are facing a personal crisis because things *are* changing. To dismiss these priests on some principle ("Wait till they die off") is a dubiously Christian attitude. Whatever relationships one chooses to have with such priests—and this depends to a large extent on one's individual ability to deal with them— we cannot dismiss them on principle. The principle, in fact, which should be at work here among Christians is that of creative love, which seeks to bring together people of even quite different views in the charity of Christ. We are committed to create communion in the real world. This is not to deny that many priests who are shaken by present-day changes certainly do look irrelevant and appear to be running scared, and that they have frequently confused a permanent commitment to the priesthood with a commitment to their own forms and expressions of priestly life. Such men, however, make up the real world; the task of priestly renewal must encompass them as well. Other priests face a crisis of weariness. They are tired of being stamped with, or having to react to an image which many people, including good Catholics, have of them. This image makes the priest the spokesman of a god who operates in a mechanical and dehumanizing way. This god threatens and punishes; he is alternately insulted, expansive, petty, disappointed and consoling—all on a godly scale. By what is in fact consistent logic, the priest who is this god's accomplice is thought to be removed from secular experience and from any worthwhile religious sensibility. People maintain their image of this god mainly by not thinking about it much one way or the other. They thereby perpetuate for the priest an irritating situation in which he feels that his quite normal capacity for friendship, for secular wisdom or for talented service is either suspect or neglected. In short, many priests wilt under constant exposure to the small thoughts of supposedly intelligent and successful people on the subject of religion.

This is not to deny that the modern priest can himself be too easily impressed by the accomplishments and style of the secular humanist. There is a clerical naïveté that finds integrity and efficiency at work everywhere except in the Church. Nor is it to claim that priests have been blameless in their assessment of the secular dimension of religious faith. Many have themselves embraced the image of the dehumanized god and have taught it to others. Many too, cling to a sterile past which they confuse with Tradition. Modern man rightly debunks their claim of divine backing for the status quo.

If we examine carefully the various situations which have given rise to the present crisis in priestly vocations, we will find one underlying assumption of the priest which makes him extremely vulnerable. To understand and to formulate correctly this central assumption will go a long way to help us understand what a priest is and what Christ meant him to be; for it is at the point of his greatest vulnerability that his real identity becomes apparent. What, then, is the priest's central conviction

81

which sustains him and at the same time imperils him? We would define it as the belief that *love is possible in all directions and that he, the priest, indicates that love in a unique, public way.* That is why we have chosen to characterize the priesthood as a "simple reminder."

This means, therefore, that the priest is not a kind of super-sacristan whom we have described adequately once we have said that "he performs cultic acts." This characterization is accurate enough in an external way, but no priesthood is sufficiently explained simply by noting what it does externally. We must, therefore, as a second point, explore the priest's inner motivation. Here we will normally find a conscious identification with the priesthood of Christ, a relationship that is not always evident. Seeing a priest in a parish involved at every level of human problems and activities (family, business, sport, study, social services, education, politics) tends to obscure the relationship to Christ which is central to his thinking on the priesthood. Yet a moment's reflection will show that other members of the geographical parish, Catholic or not, might be equally or more involved than the priest in the problems and activities enumerated. Hence such activities do not uniquely characterize him, nor do they offer us the key to his motivation. Neither can we admit that the expenditure of time, energy, and talent on the Church is the unique contribution of the priest.

This point logically brings us to a consideration of how the priest looks on the priesthood of Christ. Here his thinking is guided in part by the Scriptures. The classical scriptural locus on Christ's priesthood is the Letter to the Hebrews. Unfortunately this letter presents his priesthood in the imagery of a cosmic liturgy, with confusing references to late-Jewish temple practices. We find it difficult to cut through the scenario to the central affirmations. And yet, this letter and the other scriptural data define Christ's priesthood precisely by seeing it as a break with the normal way in which men understood priesthood up to that time. A key aspect of Christ's priesthood in the New Testament is the common bond between Christ and other men which his priesthood presupposes. Common ties of flesh, blood, suffering, trial, and temptation are absolutely basic to the reality of his priesthood (Heb. 2, 14; 4, 15). For these ties are what make Christ merciful, faithful, and compassionate to men (2, 17–18). They also allow us to describe Christ's love as one which moves in all directions, to all men and in all aspects of human life. He is almost greedy in the interests of men (Heb. 1, 2; 2, 8). He pre-tastes death for them to show them how ultimately harmless death is (Heb. 2, 9; 2, 15). He is the prayer-man. He lives to take their part before God (Heb. 7, 25). All these qualities offer a more accurate description of Christ's priesthood than does his physical dying; they supply the essential motivation for his sacrificial death. Where they are missing, as in some elements of the Jewish priesthood of his day, priesthood becomes meaningless. And indeed the laws and commandments of the Jewish priesthood are rejected by Christ to the extent that that priesthood no longer witnesses to God's compassionate concern for men (Heb. 7, 12; 7, 18; 8, 13; Mt. 12, 5; Lk. 10, 31; Jn. 17, 23).

Today's priest, then, tries to capture in his own life some of the motivation that Christ the priest had. He tries to share Christ's kind of love for men—love in all directions. But is this not true of all Christians? We have not yet determined what specifically sets the priest apart. To do so, we must consider one further aspect of Christ's priesthood: its communal and public nature.

The logic of Christ's kind of love led him, as he knew it would, to a central act of death and resurrection. It was not that his love was limited to his dying and rising. At every point we must remember that Christ lived, worked, and spoke in the towns

83

and cities he knew and loved. In the central act of dying and rising, however, the full dimensions of his love for men appear. He defines, in an *absolute* and *human* fashion, the possibilities and the validity of human love, as well as the validity of all that he had done *in the city*. What we wish to emphasize here is that his total priesthood was carried through with the specific needs and concerns of his small community of followers in mind. He led them gradually towards his passion and resurrection. In innumerable concrete situations he taught them, served them, formed and forged them: he allowed for their doubts, their gross ignorances, their selfish expectations. He adapted himself to what he can reasonably expect from them by way of belief, outlook, and adherence. The unfolding of *his priesthood,* then, was determined by the needs of the small community he was forming and with whom he was dealing. More than that, Christ wished to communicate to all men, through this small community, the nature and extent of his Father's love for men. He wanted the world to know!

Now when Christ had "gone," when he was no longer visibly present to the community, or when the original members of the community had come and gone, where was there to be a public unifying version, in or out of the community, of his kind of love? Again, where would there be room, in or out of the community, for a gradually developing realization and acceptance of God's love for men? (The very fact that God's love provided for such a gradual realization is one of the greatest indications that his love is man-centered, that it leaves room for what is historical, evolving, becoming, creative, both in the individual and in society itself.)

We are tempted to answer these questions by saying that public witness of Christ's progressive love is found in the lives of individual Christians themselves, that their lives provide the only valid public gesture which insures the continuity of the

84

Word and the action of Christ in history. Or we might be inclined to say that the Word preserved in the scriptural writings is a sufficient guarantee of the kind of continuing public witness that we need. But is this enough? Will the full dimensions and stature of his kind of commitment to men be guarded in a sufficiently tangible fashion without the reminding gesture of priesthood? The history and the sociology of communities indicate rather the need for a more specific kind of gesture, one which is more expressive than the written word, one that is more pointed or focussed than the day-by-day lives of the community members.

It is from this viewpoint that we are led to conclude that the priest becomes the community's public reminder of the word and action of Christ. By instituting this sacrament Christ attached to the community's needs and desires his efficacious promise to be present in the Word and action which they have received and *wish to perpetuate* through the priest. The human values, then, which are affirmed in the Christian priesthood are complex: there is, on the part of the community, a need and willingness to tell the story over again to itself and to re-enact its central action; there is, on the part of Christ, the effective willingness to respect this human need of the community; there is, on the part of the priest, a basic willingness to serve the developing community as its self-reminder; further, a fascination and respect for the community's founder is at the heart both of his willingness to serve and of the community's invitation to him to serve; finally, the priest is bound by common ties of need and aspiration to the members of the community whose gesture of reminding he is.

In the Christian community, these human values are strained to the extreme. The community is potentially the world. The common lot which the priest shares with others is one of sin, of futile good wishes, of meek failure, or of pure selfishness, but

85

also a common bond of hope and belief and love of love in all directions. The priest who responds to the community's invitation to recall for it *its* ideal finds himself at the service of what is almost an impossible (to believe and execute) love: Christ's love. To deliver Christ's lines without sounding too hypocritical, to keep up Christ's memory when, because of *our* own myopic mistrust, that memory often seems to condemn *us* more than it consoles us, to be called upon to recount a story by a community that often loses interest after a few chapters—this is a terrible, or a wonderful thing. The priestly gesture can so easily turn into a posture, a sign that has been jarred awry or gone rusty, a pointer that shakes in the hand, even a betrayal. But if Paul says that *we* are saved in hope, then we must be priests in hope, too. We must be convinced that the gesture is worth making.

We must remember that the need and desire for such a "reminder" is found in the community as a whole. It is not Christ's need: nor is it only the priest's personal need. Hence priests are made, as it were, by public demand. (This is perhaps why people get just about the kind of priests they deserve.) By this we mean that the community, presumably in full agreement with the necessity of the sort of gesture of self-reminding, invites some of its members to perform the task. Priests, therefore, are not substitutes for the community, but reminders; not so much mediators for the community, but reminders, in the sacrifice, of the one mediator Christ; not even particularly great lovers of the community, but voices that repeat for the community the good news and the absolution pronounced by Christ. Let no one give the priest roles that do not, in the revelation of Christ, really belong to him.

In his function of reminding the community, at its request, of the kind of love that Christ the priest first showed, the priest must spell out all over again what Christ's priesthood was all about. He must reconstruct the main actions of Christ's priesthood. This rewording and reproduction of Christ's priesthood is done, of course, primarily in the sacrifice, in the preaching of the Word, and in the sacraments. These activities are not accidental to the priest's ministry; they identify him in the deepest sense. It is in them above all that the priest answers the invitation of the community (ultimately the invitation of Christ) to tell the story of Christ's love over again and to re-enact it in the sacrifice and the absolution.

In calling the priest a "reminder" we presuppose that the Word and the sacrifice and absolution are efficacious apart from the moral and psychological integrity of individual priests (though not apart from the priest's willingness to represent the community's belief). But this is simply to say that Christ has made himself available to men in still another magnificent gesture; or that Christ's devotedness is greater than our powers of betrayal, distraction, and failure; or that he makes his presence felt where perhaps it is not always welcome; or that his is ultimately the only expression of human love in all directions that is held by no barriers. Our point, then, is not to defend the efficacy of the sacraments or the inspiration of the Word, but to describe that human action to which Christ attaches his promise of grace, and to capture that aspect of a priest's calling which will give him a basic understanding of himself in the Church.

By thus characterizing the priest, have we so restricted his service to the Christian community that we have thereby cut him off from the secular world to which many modern priests feel such a strong sense of responsibility? We are familiar with the trials of the priest-workers (worker-priests, if this will solve anything) in other countries. Seminarians express the desire to acquire a specialization, often in a secular field, if their priesthood is to be effective. Others, in the tradition of Paul, want to maintain a spiritual independence by earning their own liveli-

87

hood. No one wants to be "kept" in any sense of the word. On the other hand, priests who are engaged in secular tasks often feel disjointed in these undertakings, as though they were not "priestly" enough. What can we conclude about the priest's role in the secular city?

Part of the problem is to weigh the importance of the priest's role within the community against the fact that the community, the Church, has a mission to the secular city. Because the priest preaches the Word and administers the sacraments for the Church, it seems that people in the Church have acquired a prior right to his energies and that the priest's primary role is within the community. The community, however, does not hear the Word or live its life in a void. Is is at every point rooted in the city. Hence the expression "primary role" tends to become meaningless when we look at the Church as a movement into the world.

These are not simply academic and airy distinctions. Is the priest to get involved in the secular city only when the community fails to do so? Or is the city his natural habitat from which he has somehow become a stranger? Certainly, people resent his presence in some of the great secular movements of our times. Up to the present, the priest has been visibly and almost totally attached to his function of exercising the community's cult. He lives in a rectory near the liturgical and sacramental center of the community. His wardrobe designates him as a representative of that community rather than as one who has a job to do in the secular city. His training equips him with the in-language of his community. But the pattern is changing. The priest wants to live in an apartment; he wants to dress normally; he wants no part of a curious curial lingo. Is this changing pattern a sign that the priest today wants to neglect or betray his "primary" commitment to the community?

Perhaps rather we are dealing with a mild, if sometimes painful, realignment of a long-standing and constantly changing relationship between priest, community, and secular city. When the world's problems were problems of sanitation, education, law, public order, recreation, or politics, the clergy, by reason of their education (perhaps by reason of their *Christian* charity?), frequently undertook leadership in these secular tasks. Such involvement was almost always contested by other Christians, so history tells us, in the name of some pietistic understanding of the Church's relationship to the world. But the clergy went ahead, to the undeniable profit of civilization. But the temptation for the clergy was to become entrenched in their secular tasks, to give them up grudgingly, to invent reasons for maintaining the status quo long after the original reasons for their involvement ceased to exist. The latter phenomenon of entrenchment has always been a problem. But it does not negate the tradition of some sort of clerical involvement in the secular city. On the contrary, involvement has been so continuous and so deep-seated in the Church that it must give the lie to those who, in the name of the faith, would keep the priest in the sacristy and limit his involvement in the secular city. Therefore, in attempting to assess the modern situation it would be historically naïve and religiously questionable (in the light of the traditional pattern of secular involvement practiced by priests) to reject new forms of priestly involvement in the secular or to show an angry unwillingness to give up tasks long ago assumed. Where is the priest to be involved in the secular city today? In civil rights movements? At the peace conferences? In education? In communications media? In the arts? In publishing? In medical research? In developing the Third World? Such questions can best be answered on the basis of local need, or individual talent or inclination, or similar considerations. We must also include the general value of mutual communication and understanding that can be developed between priests and laymen, between priests and non-Catholics,

89

when priests work side by side with these groups. This value alone is so precious that it would be worthwhile for priests to continue doing certain tasks for which, as a matter of fact, the layman is equally or better suited. The real enemy here is to deny the priest a role in the secular city because he never had *that* particular role in the past.

Where does celibacy fit into the description of priesthood given above? In what sense is the priest's celibacy connected with his role as a public reminder? Is celibacy complicating his simple gesture? This is a difficult question, in which it is often impossible to distinguish the inarticulate groans of the Spirit (Rom. 8, 27) from the equally inarticulate groans of, shall we say, another spirit.

It is generally admitted that there is no necessary connection between fidelity to what God has revealed concerning the priesthood and the current practice of mandatory celibacy in the Roman rite of the Catholic Church. Hence discussions about celibacy in its relationship to priesthood are really discussions about the *convenientia* of the present legislation. While this legislation is being defended and attacked, it would be profitable to remember that, behind this debate and affecting it, even weightier issues are involved, such as the nature and formation of ecclesiastical legislation, the permanency of ordination itself, the whole Church's appreciation of marriage and sexuality, and others. In much of the debate, moreover, the pity of the liberal for the celibate priest is as illogical as is the fear of the conservative. What is called for beyond pity and fear is cool and clear thinking about how celibacy is linked to the service of public reminder that the priest performs in the community.

Now it seems difficult to deny that, generally speaking, the priest has more time, mobility, and independence for his function of community reminder and focus if he is not married. Arguments against celibacy, therefore, usually concern rather the confidence the celibate priest can instill, and his effectiveness as a reminder of Christ's love. Is is often said that lay people today find it difficult to have confidence in the judgment and advice of the priest because their own problems center about living the Christian life in the married state, of which the priest has no personal experience. Such statements are difficult to evaluate. On the one hand, it is true that there is no substitute for experience. On the other hand, one wonders whether the same mentality is at work in the above complaint that would also, for example, claim that the priest cannot speak objectively about fair housing for Negroes because he has no property or family to "defend." It is the experience of many priests that the problems married people have frequently are not problems that require them to learn from anyone what to *do*. They know what to do already, and the priest who offers "answers" risks misinterpreting his whole relationship with them. Most often, it is priests with an exaggerated notion of the priest as an authority figure who suffer most when they "cannot" give people the answers people seem to want. People need rather to talk to someone whom they can trust and who can sympathize with them. In general, do they trust each other the way they trust a priest? Again we have a question of fact. It is at least arguable that the basis of people's trust in the priest stems in large part from his celibacy, which is a *sign* of his commitment to them. The sympathy which people seek is not so specific as to demand a similar pattern of life in their listeners, but demands rather someone who accepts them as persons, as valued in themselves,—and someone who can communicate this acceptance to them. The priest does not win the trust of the people only on the basis of his personality, virtue, or talent, but also by the fact that he has been willing publicly

91

to report and register the love of Christ and has made his celibacy a gesture of this willingness.

On the other hand, it can be argued that the priest has no real opportunity to learn what human love is because he does not participate in the tangible, body-and-soul kind of love that is found only in marriage. Yet many married people remain utterly impervious to the implications of their own union. Moreover, Christ himself did not marry, and only those whose thinking is cryptically docetist or apolinarist would find this point irrelevant. The priest must preach the good news, which means that he must demythologize it in that basic and traditional sense of showing how it speaks from start to finish of the love of God for men. He must also mediate the forgiveness of Christ in the sacrament of penance, and in this encounter he must learn well the dimensions and nuances of love. For some individuals it is probably true that marriage would improve the efficiency of their ministry, but here we are speaking in terms not of time, energy, or mobility, but of the inner qualifications that, practically speaking, a man needs if he is to stand for the kind of love which Christians esteem and celebrate in their Word and sacraments.

Human love between a man and a woman remains, therefore, for the priest an all important analogy for understanding God's love for men. Its concrete and immediate quality could be a way for the priest to understand better "the holy city, a new Jerusalem, come down out of heaven from God, like a bride dressed and ready to meet her husband" (Rev. 21, 22).

We have tried in this chapter to pare away to a stark, simple structure the figure of the priest. It is our hope that the understanding of priesthood which we offer here succeeds in doing two things. First, in protecting the priest against certain alien roles in which people today try to cast him but which he accepts at his own great risk: the holy man, the man who is alienated from the secular, the ecclesiastical bureaucrat, the substitute offering, someone with special, almost magical insight. Second, to encourage priests to cut through to the central issue of their priesthood: whether or not they think it worthwhile to make the gesture of reminder that the priesthood is. The priest is a reminder *of* the saving, secular words and actions of Christ. When he makes his gesture of reminding or, more properly, when he becomes that gesture, his faith tells him that this gesture is graced with the promise of Christ to be there, speaking again to the hearts of men and acting in their lives. He is most a priest, just as Christ is most present, when he recalls the supper that Christ gave not for his servants, but for his friends. The priest is also a reminder *for* a community of believers who are thrown together in Christ, sometimes in incredible confusion, inequality, time-serving, routine and indifference, but at other times with astonishing vitality, good humor, dedication, and peace. The priest is one with that community, in its weaknesses and in its strengths, in its reflective moments and in its mission to the world. He could do a lot worse.

7.

Celebration

Discussions about the nature of the eucharist have never been great crowd-pleasers, if we can so interpret St. John: "He taught this doctrine at Capernaum, in the synagogue. After hearing it, many of his followers said, 'This is intolerable language. How could anyone accept it?' . . . After this, many of his disciples left him and stopped going with him" (Jn. 6, 59–60, 67). The matter is further complicated by the fact that in the course of time the theology of the eucharist suffered from a tendency to canonize certain questions and answers to the neglect of others. Reformation theologians debated whether the eucharist was a sacrifice and how its sacrificial character was to be understood. They asked how we should describe the process by which Christ became really present. They gave excessive attention to measuring the minimal circumstances under which there occurs what Christians say occurs in the eucharist. The long historical concentration on these questions brings with it a greater danger, namely, that having answered these questions as best we can, we give the impression of having reached a fully satisfying synthetic view of the eucharist.

Such difficulties and many others notwithstanding, the theology of the eucharist must always remain open to new questions. In particular it must address itself to perhaps the key question which is being raised today apropos of the eucharist: in what ways does the eucharist relate to what appear to be the legitimate secular concerns of men? Here there is no question of tailoring doctrine to a pattern acceptable to modern man, but of finding a language to express the mystery of the eucharist which will satisfy—to the extent that satisfaction is possible—both the demands of revelation and the demands of people for a tangible understanding of their faith.

The apostles set great store on the fact that Christ was someone tangible in their lives. St. John, for example, spoke of the Word of God as "Something . . . that we have heard, and we have seen with our own eyes; that we have watched and touched with our hands: the Word, who is life—this is our subject. That life was made visible: we saw it and are giving our testimony . . . What we have seen and heard we are telling you so that you too may have fellowship with us" (1 Jn. 1, 1–3). We quote from St. John at this point because any talk about sacraments, and any talk about the eucharist in particular, has to be based on the conviction that what is tangible, what is seen and heard and felt, is important in the religious life of men and in their theologies of that religious life. All the changes that have been introduced in the liturgy in the past ten years have been introduced with this in mind: to make contact with men as they are, to enable them to see better, to hear better, to make more visible the reality of their faith in Christ. What, then, are we properly doing when we celebrate the eucharist? What visible and tangible gesture is taking place? This is the question that we wish to explore in this chapter.

The theologian should always begin with the observable. He is aware that the sacraments are first and foremost signs or observable symbolic actions. By "symbolic action," however, we do not mean only that Christians are doing something symbolically in their eucharist. It is obvious that they are. What is meant rather is that Christians are doing something that is itself a symbol and was itself a symbol before Christians started doing it. Christian symbolism is built out of meaningful, secular, symbolic actions which may be recognized as such even apart from any added signification given to these actions by Christ. In the case of the eucharist the prior symbolic action is something that is quite tangible. It is the simple matter of a meal. Our procedure, then, will be first to enlarge upon the secular meaning of meals; and, second, to show how the Christian eucharist is an intensification of such secular meals.

Before proceeding to this task we might remark on the benefits which flow from reflecting on the eucharist as a symbolic action, namely, a meal. If we allow the understanding of meal that is presented in this chapter, it becomes easier to see how the attitudes of the host are to be included, at a fundamental level of understanding, as part of the symbolic action of having a meal together. Accordingly, the Last Supper could readily "carry" the sacrificial attitude of Christ. Hence, too, we could conclude that the Christian eucharist which effects the presence of Christ also intends to be a sacramental presentation of Christ's sacrifice. This is in fact the conclusion reached by Eric Mascall in his work *Corpus Christi,* which throws much light on the question of the relationship between the eucharist as community meal and the eucharist as community sacrifice.

Another contemporary controversy in eucharistic theology whose resolution is furthered by stressing the fact that the eucharist is a symbolic action is that concerning transsubstantiation and transignification. The basic issue here has been: how do we best explain our belief that Christ becomes present there where, to all appearances, only bread and wine are present? The Council of Trent established transsubstantiation as a valid and necessary explanation. Some recent theologians, however, relying again on the fact that the eucharist is primarily a symbolic action, and pointing out that symbolic action as such principally concerns changes in the meaning of things (rather than in their physical

97

constitution), have offered transignification as a valid explanation. Powers' *Eucharistic Theology* has presented this matter well. He sees no contradiction in saying that the "marvelous and singular conversion" of the bread and wine into the body and blood of Christ is effected in such wise that we may call that conversion from different points of view, both transubstantiation and transignification. He laments the inability of many to *take* the point of view that would make the theology of transignification orthodox and benign.

But to return then to our main theme: the two directions our analysis will take us are (1) a consideration of the qualities which distinguish the meal as a remarkable form of human activity, and (2) an examination of the particular circumstances of the Christian meal.

It is often remarked that small children are not too keen on meals. This hardly means that the child is disinterested in eating. The child's appreciation of the meal-situation is, however, limited. When conversation begins the child exhibits its limited appreciation of this aspect of eating by squirming, fidgeting, and asking, finally, that he mercifully be excused from "the table."

An adult meal seems to imply some sort of conversation-over-food. It differs from conversation, even from engrossing conversation, in the fact that it takes place over food. Somehow, the sharing of food seems to enhance the conversation and the sharing of experience or news. It gives a special and humanly powerful setting to the asking of some bothersome question, to the revelation of some happy decision. We could probably best inform ourselves about the uniqueness of confronting each other amid the tastes and smells of food and drink by consulting the endless lines of people who crowd the doorways of the evening restaurants in our larger cities. Meals are special human occasions with their own kind of solemnity and their own way of bringing people face to face with each other.

98

Three further characteristics, moreover, seem to apply to meals. Meals come from a common somewhere; they contain an element of intense communication and comment (not necessarily in words); they lead to a common somewhere. We do not normally consider dining with complete strangers to be a meal. There is not enough of a common past to warrant the name of meal. At times, however, a dinner with strangers can turn into a meal by reason of the fact that we discover common ties in past experience which allow the context for a present communication to form. There seems to be a necessity for common human ties before separate tables can be pushed together in any meaningful way.

As for meals leading to a common somewhere, a crude instance is found in the film *Tom Jones*. To describe the intensity of comment and communication that belongs to meals, we take the example of the meal in Banuel's *Viridiana*. Viridiana is the heroine whose almsgiving is an insult to the poor, not so much because it is Christian (as many interpret Banuel) as because it veils her attempt to repress some quite human aspects of her personality. The poor people she has befriended take advantage to invade her house and stage a brawling meal. The meal becomes a bitter comment on Viridiana's altruism. There is an unspoken communication between the meals's participants; each contributes to the central insinuation of the blasphemous meal: that Viridiana's almsgiving is hateful.

Such participatory comment is intense. Meals do not necessarily bring about fellowship or warmth; they can be disturbing. Their conversation takes the participants through a spectrum of vivid human reactions such as the realization of another person's needs or interests, insight into oneself or into the meaning and direction of events, and an appreciation of the changing dimensions of life or work. This interpersonal sharing and communication is, finally, mirrored in the sharing of the same food.

99

When Christ enjoined on his followers to "do this in memory of me," he was indicating at least that they were to do this meal kind of thing. He was, further, calling for the re-enactment not just of any meal but of a Last Supper kind of meal. What dimensions, then, are added to the general characterization of meal we have given by the peculiar circumstances of the Last Supper? What was the Last Supper's common past? What was its common future to be? What intense communication and comment did it afford? In raising these questions we are in fact laying the groundwork for a threefold consideration of our own eucharistic celebration as memorial (anamnesis), as sharing (koinonia), and as anticipation of the return of Christ (1 Cor. 11, 26).

One unique aspect of the eucharistic meal consists in the fact that the bread and wine, the food, are so central. The people at a meal are usually more important than the food. But where Christ is affirmed to be present to fill the hunger of men for self-knowledge and for community, for openness and for festivity, it is understandable that interest is going to center on that encounter. Yet it remains true that Christ's promise is to be present to the Christian community as it celebrates a *meal* of bread and wine. Hence the integral picture of the eucharistic sign of the Last Supper should include a description of the meal-context itself. This context is provided by St. John, whose Gospel should be taken not simply as a sudsidiary source for understanding the eucharistic sign presented in the synoptic institution accounts, but as essential to the full description of the sacramental sign itself.

Several divisions of the Joannine narrative (chs. 13–17) are possible, and all of them would be somewhat arbitrary. So it would perhaps be better to distinguish between the significant events that took place during the Supper and the conversation proper. The former are relatively few: the washing of the feet

100

of the disciples, the departure of Judas from the room. The conversation is more nearly a monologue, since Jesus does most of the talking. Yet there are revealing interventions by Peter (13, 6. 8. 9. 36–37), by the disciple whom Jesus loved (13, 25), by Thomas (14, 5), by Philip (14, 8), and by Judas (14, 22). In the literary repetition of Chapter 14 which is found in Chapter 16 (5–33) these remarks are ascribed in a general way to "some of the disciples" (16, 17. 29–30).

What characterizes the interventions of the apostles is their irrelevance to Jesus' own train of thought. His remarks run at deep levels. They center on several themes: (1) his "going" to the Father, just as he "came" from the Father; (2) the "necessity" of this "going"; (3) the relationship of Jesus and of his followers to "the world"; (4) the role of the Paraclete in the lives of the apostles; (5) the glorification that Jesus' return to the Father will bring to Jesus personally; (6) the new commandment to love one another. With the exception of the latter exhortation to love one another the remarks of Jesus are met with confusion and questioning on the apostles' part. In fact, their one pretense at understanding Jesus (16, 29–30) is rejected by him.

One of the most obvious conclusions to be drawn from the above description of the Last Supper is that, notwithstanding the confusion and even the tension, Jesus thinks it is worthwhile celebrating with his followers. Their perfect assimilation of his mentality never becomes a pre-condition of their celebrating with him and with each other. The Last Supper is itself a point in a developing relation between Jesus and his followers and among his followers themselves.

This point unites his past association with them to their present moment of camaraderie and of eliciting and exchanging human sentiment and divine faith. Moreover, it moves them all towards an obscure future which will be marked by their own infidelity, by Jesus' absence, by their need to learn Jesus' mentality from the Paraclete, by persecution, and by the gradual fulfilling of the new commandment of charity.

The extent to which a common past is present in the Last Supper requires special comment. For Jesus himself the thought of his approaching death is central during the Last Supper. The disciples do not share his sense of imminent doom. If anything, their minds are on less worthy matters of concern. But because the approaching death is on Jesus' mind, we have to say that it fits into the celebration itself. It forms, therefore, part of the anamnesis (memorial) which he asks from his followers. Yet it is not as if Jesus looks upon his own death and wishes to "celebrate" it with any grotesque intent. He is rather celebrating with his disciples a common effort which consisted, for three years, in loving the Father and loving each other. He is celebrating, too, the acts of his Father in history which have led up to and, after their own fashion, mirrored his moment of victory in defeat. Jesus' own way of love has taken him to this moment of death. He is satisfied that he has been true to love. And he is celebrating most of all the freedom of men in the pursuit of love —which is at once his Father's greatest gift to men and the greatest act in history.

That is why the ragged and inconclusive conversation of the Last Supper does not deter Jesus from the celebration itself. He is still giving his disciples scope—scope to learn and to question and even to leave him. He is not indifferent to their future. In communicating to them their need to do *this* meal kind of thing again he advises them that their community of love needs him if it is to succeed. He indicates to them that their common future will be authentic only if it is tied to him and ties them to each other.

It is, then, this meal of Christ with his disciples which Christians do in their eucharist. Perhaps we can profit from this reflection on the observable qualities of the Last Supper in order to make such qualities central to our own eucharist. The radical humanity of this sacrament consists in the fact that it is a celebration which furthers the community begun by Christ and with Christ in baptism. Celebration is a Christian way of life, not in the sense that Christians are the only ones who celebrate human relationships, but in that they are formally and structurally committed to celebrate with each other in the face of their own ignorance and shortcomings. Moreover, Christians are to extend this hopeful view of celebration to the whole world. It is a Christian imperative to break down the excommunication of the secular, that is, to be alert to communicate to all the real possibility of celebration *in the midst of* human living.

One final remark is in order here. It would be easy to reject the above description of the eucharist as meal-celebration when it is so apparent that the mentalities and actions of Christians themselves and of men in general are such that celebration seems hypocritical. Divisions in matters of moral value and of human conduct seem too great to allow for communication, for sharing a common past or a common future. Yet it is precisely a pessimism in the face of such divisions that Christ is rejecting in instituting the eucharist. The logic of the eucharist is clear: if man cannot break bread together, then his divisions will surely undo him. In Christ the world is reminded of this simple yet awesome truth.

Epilogue

If the sacraments are the home of so much humanity, it seems only fair to inquire why it is that their secular and humanistic dimension is neglected in the lives of Christians. From one point of view, many Christians expect too little from the sacraments. They do not expect that Christ addresses himself to their condition; they think rather that his concern is solely for their extra-temporal salvation, a salvation whose content is at best obscure and at worst threatening, boring, or puzzling. From another point of view, however, Christians expect too much from the sacraments. The effectiveness of the sacraments lies in their being signs. But as we have seen, the signs which Christ makes to us in the sacraments and which we make in turn emerge from inner personal freedom and go forth to meet other freedoms in the world around us. Neither man nor God guarantees the successful use of personal freedom.

God's signs in the biblical revelation were in fact usually attached to his promise, whether that promise was to make the people of Israel great or to send a spiritual redeemer. But the biblical promise was a demanding orientation of man, a call and summons, rather than a guarantee or preview of favorable outcome. Man must hope in the promise of the sacraments and try them out in their humanistic dimensions before he can judge their humane effectiveness. We are saved here and now by the sacraments, but this salvation, like all salvation insofar as it relates to this life, must be lived out in hope. We hope that our lives will be courageous, adult, open, sexually fulfilled, of service

105

to others, congenial to the last. To give up these hopes in the face of the fact that performance lags behind belief opens the way to a denial of life itself, since life is tabulated as much by ideals as by statistics. To make empirical success the final norm of effectiveness belies the mentality of the one whose gestures sacraments basically are, namely, the ineffectual Christ who succumbs to his opposition and who cannot count even a handful of supporters in his hour of personal need.

Hence sacraments do not marshall our lives. Their structure gives scope and provides for the initiative of the believer. If some people are disappointed because sacraments are more orientation than regimentation, they should not for that reason force the sacraments to do more than they can do. Sacraments affirm that despite all there is soundness in life, in society, in married love, in death. But the Christ of the sacraments demands faith in the reality of the soundness which they promise, so that only the believer judges their effectiveness in the concrete.

If there is any unreality to the sacraments it is the benign kind of unreality which forms a part of our normal experience. "What if . . .," we say. "What if the human community we yearn for could be accomplished. What if the progress of life from adolescence to adulthood could be accompanied by concern and wisdom. What if the party could go on and the recreative conversation continue. What if the dead did not die alone. What if man could hold in his mind and in his heart the things that he once knew but often forgot." A proper understanding of the sacraments requires that we see them precisely as the affirmation of the highly unreal but equally persistent desires of men and women for a better secular life in this world.

A further general remark that we could make about the sacraments is that, as we have seen, they involve all Christians, whether they realize this fact or not, in community. It is the community that feels the weight and sadness of death and expresses a "better hope" through the last anointing. It is the community that is committed to a renewed love for the sinner, to that kind of forgiving and forgetting that is expressed in the priest's absolution. It is the community that invites the newly ordained priest to re-enact its cult and to tell the story over again. The community calls for the Spirit of maturity in the young and thereby asks for its own renewal and its own deeper insertion into the task of renewing the face of the earth. The community celebrates life and community itself at the baptism of a child. The community even enters into the private recesses of married love by affirming the incarnate presence of Christ in that love. It is the community, finally, which breaks bread at Christ's table and discovers one another there in the camaraderie and common hunger of that moment.

At a more theoretical level, where we are dealing with symbolic actions, the terminology which describes the sacramental sign in terms of its "matter" and "form" is perhaps less adequate for our understanding of what is taking place in sacraments than the terminology which recurs in this study, namely, when we spoke of the "action" of a sacrament (what we normally understand by matter and form) and the "context" of that action. Thus the action of baptism—which here means both pouring the water and saying the words—is in the context of an initiation. This context supplies much insight into the sacrament since by itself it implies that Christ and the community is convinced of the value of initiating community, of affirming life through community. The actions of the other sacraments and the contexts of those sacraments could be analyzed in similar fashion. The context of confirmation is an initiation into adult community. The context of the anointing of the sick is a delegation to the sick. The context of confession and absolution is conversation. The context of priesthood is the community's acquiring someone who is specifically directed to recall and to replay for it its word. The

107

context of marriage is the Christian community's own standard of human love. The context of the eucharist is the meal-conversation. These several contexts manifest the mentality of Christ and of his followers and an appreciation of them is essential to an understanding of the sacraments.

There is, finally, an ecumenical concern in the theology of sacraments as presented in this study. Certainly, other Churches than the Roman Catholic Church *do* many of the things that are described here as sacramental actions. Do these Churches affirm that Christ has attached a formal promise to be present to these actions? Are these Churches structurally committed to such actions? To what extent is a refusal to *call* a sacrament what one *does* a barrier to ecumenical unity? Vatican Council II has, to some extent, valorized, for itself at least, the structures and works of other Christian communities. It seems to us that there is much hope that one day the sacramental life of all Christians may also become, in word and in deed, a unified sign of Christ's presence to the world.